The Trans-Caucasian Campaign of the Turkish Army Under Omer Pasha
by Laurence Oliphant

Address:
HardPress
8345 NW 66TH ST #2561
MIAMI FL 33166-2626
USA
Email: info@hardpress.net

41

THE STORY

OF THE

CAMPAIGN OF SEBASTOPOL.

WRITTEN IN THE CAMP.

BY LIEUT.-COL. E. B. HAMLEY,
CAPTAIN R.A.

ORIGINALLY PUBLISHED IN BLACKWOOD'S MAGAZINE.

LIST OF ILLUSTRATIONS.

OPINIONS OF THE PRESS.

"We strongly recommend this 'Story of the Campaign' to all who would gain a just comprehension of this tremendous struggle. Of this we are perfectly sure, it is a book unlikely to be superseded. Its truth is of that simple and sterling character which is sure of an immortal existence; nor is it paying the gallant author too high a compliment to class this masterpiece of military history with the most precious of those classic records which have been bequeathed to us by the great writers of antiquity, who took part in the wars they have described."—*Press.*

"The narrative is clear and forcible. It often brings a stronger sense of the reality before the mind than the 'graphic' paintings of the 'Correspondent;' and combines with the story of action an idea of purpose, and of the causes of success or failure."—*Spectator.*

"The readers of *Blackwood's Magazine* are all familiar with the spirited sketches transmitted from month to month from a tent in the Crimea, for the information of the British public; and most welcome to them will be the present volume, which embodies them all in one consecutive tale, and adds to their interest both by the picturesque illustrations which adorn it, and by the name of the writer on the title-page, imparting to the narrative a degree of authenticity which it could not have as an anonymous production."—*John Bull.*

"One of the best existing accounts of the entire campaign. The style of the book is wonderful, considering that it was all written in camp, in the intervals of military duty. . . . Opinions are rarely expressed, but all the facts are shown in such sequence as generally to exhibit, in the most striking way, the marked features of the campaign."—*Examiner.*

W. BLACKWOOD & SONS, EDINBURGH AND LONDON.

MESSR. ZUTHER, DEL.

M.& N. HANHART. IMP.

THE BATTLE OF THE INGOUR.

THE

TRANS-CAUCASIAN CAMPAIGN

OF

THE TURKISH ARMY

UNDER

OMER PASHA

𝔄 𝔓ersonal 𝔑arrative

BY

LAURENCE OLIPHANT

Author of " The Russian Shores of the Black Sea,"
" Minnesota and the Far West," &c.

WILLIAM BLACKWOOD AND SONS
EDINBURGH AND LONDON
MDCCCLVI

The Author of this Work notifies that he reserves the right of authorising translation of it.

83*23

CONTENTS.

ILLUSTRATIONS.

WOODCUTS.

---

* From Drawings taken on the spot by Herr Zuther, Omer Pasha's artist.

ERRATA.

Page 29, line 2, *for* " a hundred" *read* " two hundred."

,, 31, ,, 6, *for* " blazing" *read* "playing."

INTRODUCTORY CHAPTER.

THE following pages had just passed through the Press, when I received some drawings from Herr Zuther, the artist who accompanied Omer Pasha upon our late campaign; and I was induced to postpone the publication of this volume until they could be added to it. In the mean time the papers relative to the defence and capitulation of Kars were laid upon the table of the House of Commons; and I avail myself of the interval which this delay has occasioned, to insert an introductory chapter, as the Blue Book, while it confirms in every particular the views and statements I had previously made, throws so much additional light upon the subject, and clears up so many points which were before involved in mystery, that any examina-

a

tion into its contents is invested with the deepest interest. In the latter half of that volume the various projects for the relief of Kars by a succouring army are discussed at length. The reasons which induced the Turkish government to propose, and our own government at last to concur in, a Transcaucasian campaign, are set forth in detail ; and the causes of that delay which retarded the operation until so late a period of the year that success was impossible, fill many melancholy but instructive pages.

From the first part of the Blue Book it would appear that the Turkish government had been most remiss in neglecting to send supplies as well as reinforcements to Kars. At last, on the 28th of June, Lord Stratford writes, " that it is some consolation to me to find that, even at this eleventh hour, the necessity of listening to my advice and sending off reinforcements without further delay, is recognised." Here, then, when the summer is half over, and the Russian army has already got under canvass beneath the walls of Kars, the Turkish government for the first time awakes to the danger.

Then follows the reaction usual in such cases, and the Ottoman cabinet now becomes nervously anxious to avert those disastrous consequences which their own culpable apathy and indifference have entailed.

There is one preliminary to relieving a besieged town which is indispensable : it is, that you must first find your army. The excited imagination and inventive genius of the Turkish Minister promptly produced for Lord Stratford's consideration the following receipt for concocting a relieving army : Of Vivian's Contingent take 20,000, stir up with it 3000 of Beatson's Bashi-Bazouks, throw in the Batoum garrison, garnish with 2000 Albanians, add 5000 drawn from Bulgaria, and season with Egyptian regular cavalry and Tunisian horse. The result to be 43,000 men, and General Vivian in command. No wonder that Lord Stratford, in sending this proposal to Lord Clarendon, adds, " Your Lordship will easily comprehend my embarrassment." Their destination is to be Mingrelia, and ultimately Tiflis. Lord Stratford hesitates in his approval of the scheme, consults General Vivian, and refers home. General Vivian " does not entertain a

doubt of the advantage of the proposed measure,
provided it can be efficiently arranged ;" but
meantime he contents himself with a few
prudent and cautious observations, and sends
in a memorandum of the means of conveyance
and requirements of an army of 25,000 men,
which must have rather astonished the Turkish
authorities.   There is one item of 15,000 horses,
5000 of which were for provisions alone—doubtless no more than necessary, but about three
times more than the number furnished to Omer
Pasha.   With 5000 provision-horses we should
have reached Kutais easily.   Meantime Lord
Clarendon, horror-struck at the proposal of the
Porte, objects in the strongest terms to
throwing on an enemy's coast 40,000 men,
" hurriedly collected from various quarters, imperfectly disciplined, doubtfully armed and
equipped, and as yet unorganised."   Indeed, it
would not be difficult to imagine the fate of
this scratch-pack in Mingrelia.   The transport
corps formed on the spot would have broken
down, and the contingent, imperfectly organised, would first have become hungry, then
discontented, then demoralised.   The Bashi-
Bazouks would never have been hungry; they

would have carried ruin and desolation through-out the country, and ultimately pronounced open war against the Albanians.   As the Ba-toum garrison, numbered at twelve thousand, did not effectively exist, it is needless to specu-late upon their probable proceedings.   The five thousand drawn from Bulgaria, being veteran troops, would have bade General Vivian a respectful adieu, and, retreating in an orderly manner to Redoute Kaleh, have made their escape as they best could ; while the Egyptians and Tunisians would have died from cold, as most of them have since done.

But while the idea of sending an army thus formed into Transcaucasia was insane, the pro-ject of a campaign in those provinces was full of merit ; and it is but fair to give the Turkish government credit for originating this plan of operations.   They invited Lord Stratford to a conference for the purpose of considering it.   The Grand Vizier, the Seras-kier, Fuad Pasha, and General Mansfield, were present at this meeting ; and Lord Stratford, in his despatch to Lord Claren-don alluding to it, says : " It was clear to all present that, whether the Russians besieged

or turned Kars, the Turkish army required
an effort to be made for its relief with all
practicable despatch; and that of three possible
modes of acting for that purpose, the only one
likely to prove effective was an expedition by
Kutais into Georgia.   To send reinforcements
by Trebizond would be at best a palliative."

Her Majesty's Government, however, was
of opinion "that the wiser course would
be to send reinforcements to the rear of
the Turkish army, instead of sending an expedition to the rear of the Russian army."
The reason given being, that the distance from
Trebizond to Erzeroum is less than from Redoute Kaleh to Tiflis; but as it was quite
unnecessary to get to Tiflis, that seems hardly
to the point.   With a properly organised commissariat, the Pass of Suramm is attainable in
a far shorter time from Redoute Kaleh than
Erzeroum is from Trebizond, and can be
reached by an excellent Russian post-road
instead of an impracticable mountain-path;
and there can be no doubt that had Omer
Pasha occupied that pass, he would have
caused far more uneasiness to Mouravieff than
if he had advanced to Erzeroum ; while, if

(as the result showed would have been the case) Kars had fallen before he could reach it, he would, to give his own opinion, as expressed by Colonel Simmons in a despatch to Lord Clarendon, " have found himself inferior in force to the enemy, and therefore unable, his army being fatigued and diminished by a long and difficult march, to reconquer the lost ground ; whereas, by moving upon Kutais, the enemy, whose principal force is in the neighbourhood of Kars, would be constrained to retire a large portion of that force, not having other troops available in front of Tiflis to cover that town and his communication with it.　If the Pasha could, by a rapid movement in sufficient force, gain Kutais and seize the Suramm Pass, which is the key of the Tiflis road, he considers he would then be in a position, according to circumstances, to act against Tiflis, or unite his force by Akhiska with the army at Kars, if that place should not in the mean time have fallen."　It was also known that between Redoute Kaleh and Tiflis there were not above fifteen thousand Russian troops.

　　It is to be regretted, therefore, that our Government, while deprecating the employment of

such a force as the one originally proposed
by the Porte, should not have expressed approval of the scheme in a strategical and
political point of view. "Her Majesty's Government," says Lord Stratford, "not only
withhold the Contingent, but express a decided
preference for the alternative of sending reinforcements to Erzeroum by the way of Trebizond. This opinion is not adopted by the Porte,
or indeed by any official or personal authority here. The Seraskier, Omer Pasha, General Guyon, our own officers, as far as I have
means of knowing, agree with the Porte and
the French embassy in preferring a diversion
on the side of Redoute Kaleh, as offering
better chances of success." This difference of
opinion paralysed all efforts for the time. A
whole month had already elapsed since the
subject was first broached by Lord Stratford.
Omer Pasha had, immediately upon being
apprised of the state of affairs, urgently applied to take his army from the Crimea into
Asia ; but the coldness with which the project was received by our Government, and
the determined opposition given to it in the
Crimea, condemned to utter inaction a well-

organised army and a skilful general. Nothing could be decided upon. "Meanwhile," says Lord Stratford in concluding his despatch, " the advices from Kars are not encouraging ; and time, of precious value, is unavoidably wasted in doubt and uncertainty."

It was, however, perhaps scarcely to be expected that, in the absence of those minute geographical details which are necessary to a consideration of the question, our Government should have preferred the more simple operation ; and every credit must be given for the promptness with which, upon arriving at a correct appreciation of the superior advantages of this campaign, they at once laid Omer Pasha's proposal, as approved by them, before the French government. But in order to understand the origin of the new complications which were now about to arise, we must delay for a little, and, going back a fortnight in time, change the scene to the Crimea.

On the 12th of July, Omer Pasha had requested the Allied generals to meet him in council on the 14th, to consider the expediency of an Asiatic campaign, for the relief of Kars. At this conference Omer Pasha explained to the

Generals the information he had received from his government, relative to the Russian forces in Asia, and the position of matters there generally,—offering, however, to remain for any decided operation in immediate contemplation, for which the presence of his army was necessary. "The Generals and the Admirals," says Colonel Simmons, in his account of the conference, "having received no information from their respective Ambassadors at Constantinople, which should lead them to believe that the affairs of Asia were in that precarious state in which Omer Pasha, from the information he had received from his government, believed them to be, decided that in the absence of such information they could give no opinion upon the subject." Alluding to which afterwards, Lord Stratford tells Lord Clarendon "that the state of the army at Kars was made known to the British Commander-in-Chief by General Williams himself."

Omer Pasha left the Crimea on the following day and proceeded to Constantinople, in order to press the matter there. He was accompanied by Lieutenant-Colonel Suleau, who was the bearer of a letter from General Simpson ; and was also charged by General Pelissier with a mission to the French Ambassador on the same subject. This officer, General Simpson informs us, was sent "ostensibly for the purpose of restoring his health." We are allowed a peep into the missive of which this invalid was the bearer. General Simpson tells Lord Stratford that the arguments used by Omer Pasha "failed to produce any effect on the minds of the other members of the conference, who all, without exception, entertain the strongest objection to the withdrawal of any troops from the Crimea at this moment." "Finally," says General Simpson, "I earnestly, therefore, beg your Excellency to use your powerful influence with the Porte, to cause our opinion to prevail over that of his Highness ; for great public interests are at stake, and serious consequences might result from his success." The General was perfectly right : a very serious consequence—to wit, the salvation of Kars— would have resulted from it. This letter will enable us to guess what the tenor of General Pelissier's mission to his Ambassador probably was. The effect of that mission is apparent in a telegraphic despatch from Lord Cowley to Lord

Clarendon, in answer to one from our Foreign Minister, approving of Omer Pasha's proposal as communicated to him by Lord Stratford, and hoping "that the Government of the Emperor will concur in it."

" Count Walewski foresees objections to the proposal contained in your despatch of yesterday. He will submit it, however, to the Emperor, and hopes to give me his Majesty's answer on Saturday."

An earnest and well-written despatch from Lord Clarendon to Lord Cowley, upon the same subject, receives the telegraphic answer that " the French government will not oppose the projected expedition into Asia Minor (they never thought of going to Asia Minor), under Omer Pasha, provided that the numbers of the Turkish contingent before Sebastopol are not diminished ;" which is forwarded on for Omer Pasha's benefit, who naturally finds a difficulty in taking his army away from the Crimea and not diminishing the force there. But it is proposed that the Contingent shall replace them in equal force. Omer Pasha is only allowed some of his troops. He, not unreasonably, wishes them to be the best, who are vegetating at Kamara ; but the Contingent are ordered to replace those at Eupatoria, which are his worst : so he objects again. Then they are to go to Balaklava, when the whole matter seems so nearly settled, that the French government gets alarmed at the responsibility it has assumed, and Lord Cowley telegraphs to Lord Clarendon to the following effect : " The Emperor has no objection to the removal of the Turkish troops from Balaklava, and to their being replaced by others, provided that the Allied commanders-in-chief have no objection ; but he will not take on himself the responsibility of saying more. Under these circumstances, I send the telegraphic despatch to General Simpson, inserting after the word ' Asia,' ' provided that you and General Pelissier have no objection.'" The latter has the strongest possible objection, and General Simpson agrees of course. In their opinion, the safety of the whole Allied army, consisting of upwards of 150,000 French, English, and Sardinian troops, depends upon the presence of 20,000 of Omer Pasha's soldiers. If they were replaced by the same number of General Vivian's, they were not prepared to say what fatal consequences might not follow. This is probably the highest compliment that was ever paid to so small a force.

Meantime August has already drawn to a close, when the matter is thus left to the discretion of Generals Pelissier and Simpson. During the whole of the following month, one most critical to the garrison of Kars, the Turkish army cook their rice, drink their coffee, and smoke their pipes at Kamara. On the 16th of August Colonel Simmons writes—" Omer Pasha doubts if the expedition will now be in time to save the garrison of Kars ; but if not, it will at any rate prevent the enemy from establishing himself in the government of Erzeroum," &c. It was not till *two* months after this that the last detachment of the Turkish army left the Crimea. Nobody had now any doubts as to the propriety of the campaign. The elaborate examination into its merits by Fuad Pasha, Colonel Simmons, and Omer Pasha, leaves no question as to its correctness in a military point of view. " It can hardly be denied," says Lord Stratford, " that the scheme is plausible. The military authorities here, in so far as I have access to them, are decidedly favourable to it." Mr

Brant, the consul at Erzeroum, whose advice is certainly not always consistent, says, in one place, " I shall be very anxious to hear of the landing of an adequate force at Redoute Kaleh, as Kars by that event alone might, I hope, be saved." And even General Williams says, " Should her Majesty's Government and its Allies determine on making Trebizond the base of future operations against Georgia, I still trust that an immediate and powerful demonstration will be made by a Turkish army from Redoute Kaleh." On the 1st of September that officer again writes : " The most is made of our provisions. The soldier is reduced to half allowance of bread and meat, or rice and butter —sometimes one hundred drachams of biscuit, nothing besides. No money. Mussulman population (three thousand Rifles) will soon be reduced to starvation ; Armenians are ordered to quit the town to-morrow. No barley ; scarcely any forage. Cavalry reduced to walking skeletons, and sent out of garrison ; artillery-horses soon the same. How will the field-pieces be moved after that ? The apathy of the superior officers is quite distressing. We can hold out two months more. What is being done for the relief of this army ?" This important question is answered, if we refer to Colonel Simmons' despatch to the Earl of Clarendon, dated three weeks later (September 21), from the Crimea : "Up to the present time General Pelissier has not signified his assent to the departure for Asia of any more of the Ottoman troops now stationed here." Two thousand had been allowed to depart three days before. Sebastopol had fallen a fortnight previous to this. The principal use of a portion of the Turkish army had been to hold some lines at Baidar. It had never been employed in the trenches, nor was it engaged in the siege. It was now becoming an actual encumbrance and embarrassment to the Allied forces, encamped in so limited a space. "It would appear to be most desirable," says Colonel Simmons, " for the interest of the Allied troops now here that they should depart." Again, " General Simpson has informed me that he sees no objection to their departure. The only obstacle therefore seems to be, that the assent of General Pelissier and the French government has not been given." Here, then, we are enabled, for the first time, to arrive at some definite conclusion as to the immediate and proximate cause of the fall of Kars.

Whatever may have been the neglect of the Turkish government in the first instance, with regard to the commissariat of the garrison—how distressing soever the apathy and corruption of the Ottoman officials may then have been—there can be no doubt that, in spite of all these evil and disastrous influences, had the French government entertained the proposition of Omer Pasha when it was first pressed upon them by Lord Clarendon, instead of leaving it to the generals in the Crimea, Kars would never have been taken. There is indeed a very fair probability that, even at the eleventh hour, when Sebastopol had fallen, and General Simpson stated that he had no further need for the presence of the Turkish army, if General Pelissier had then authorised its departure, instead of three weeks later, that unfortunate garrison would have been saved. But whether this was so or not, it is certain that, in that case, the Turkish army would have been at this moment in possession of the Pass of Suramm, from whence the fertile valley of the Kur, and the cities of Gori and Tiflis, lying at its feet,

b

would offer an inviting field of operations for a spring campaign ; while those four populous provinces of Imeritia, Mingrelia, Gouriel, and Abkhasia, wrested from the dominion of Russia, would have furnished Lord Clarendon with the power of demanding from that Empire more than an equivalent for her recent success.

So far, then, the publication of the Blue Book has indeed been most valuable.   There is, however, one point of great importance upon which it is silent ; and in default of any information thereupon, it would be imprudent to hazard a decided opinion as to the real and ultimate cause of the late disaster in Asia.   We learn from its pages that one General proposed to take an army to the relief of Kars, and the reasons are fully stated which induced him to make the proposition, and confidently to predict success.   We are further informed who those Generals were who opposed the prosecution of this design ; but we are nowhere enlightened as to their motives for so doing.   When, however, we remember the serious consequences which this refusal involved, and the high military authorities from whom it emanated, we can scarcely allow ourselves to doubt the correctness of the decision at which they arrived. At the same time, the considerations by which they were influenced must have been so weighty and important that it is only a pardonable curiosity if (now that nothing is to be feared from their disclosure) we may be permitted to inquire what they were. " It is unnecessary," says Lord Stratford, " to fill up the only lacuna which appears in either the statement (on the measures taken for the relief of Kars, drawn up by General Mansfield) or the abstract (of correspondence on the same subject by Count Pisani). I am content to leave the circumstances, which are there passed over, to your Lordship's recollection and sense of justice."

Passing, then, from the sea of conjecture here thrown open to us, I shall now endeavour to give some account of the campaign which, at the end of last autumn, the Turkish army was allowed to undertake, and its results in a political and military point of view.

THE
TRANS-CAUCASIAN CAMPAIGN
OF THE
TURKISH ARMY.

CHAPTER I.

HE only who knows what it is, night after night, to court sleep in defiance of the thundering of a hundred cannon—to be ever conscious, in his dreams of home, of the incessant whistle of shot and shell—and to be generally roused from a rickety stretcher by the explosion of a mine, can fully appreciate the comfort of a quiet cabin far removed from these disturbing influences, where the shrill pipe of the boatswain, or the morning sun gleaming in at the port-hole, remind him that another day of *dolce far niente* has dawned. It was upon a

lovely morning in September last year, and
only a week prior to the fall of Sebastopol,
that I looked from the deck of H.M.S. "Highflyer" upon the magnificent range which skirts
the southern shores of the Crimea, where wooded dells wind among the mountains, and vines
and olives clothe its slopes, and white chateaux
gleam from out the dark foliage of the over-
shadowing horse-chestnut, and, towering over
all, the Tchatir Dagh abruptly rises and throws
its sombre shade over the sunny landscape.
Rounding Cape Takli, whose friendly beacon
no longer exists to guide the benighted ma-
riner, we soon after drop anchor beneath the
newly - constructed fortifications of St Paul,
where the British flag would indicate that the
white tents which crown the hill are those of
our own soldiers, even were the tartan trews
of a Highland regiment not so clearly discern-
ible.   But when we land to inspect the fort,
we find ourselves surrounded as well by
Turks and French, who here occupy such a
position as to render any hostile movement,
except with a larger body of troops than the
Russians could spare, unavailing.

It is about two miles across a gently undu-

lating steppe from here to Kertch, the well-
built mansions of which, from this distance,
look as handsome and substantial as though it
were still a flourishing mercantile emporium.
As we enter, however, the delusion rapidly van-
ishes, and it is painful to witness a ruin and
desolation so universal. Three years ago I had
walked along the quay in the midst of a throng
of gay promenaders. Fashionable ladies, es-
corted by well-dressed beaux, strolled by the
water-side, or lingered round the band which
played in the garden opposite the governor's
house ; for it was a Sunday afternoon in autumn, and all the world was enjoying the delicious air, which at this time of year renders
the Crimean climate so particularly delightful.
Then the market-place was full of bustle and
activity ; camel-carts and Tartar waggons, with
scraggy ponies, crowded the streets ; and Russian officials stalked pompously about, with
that dignified air which increases in intensity,
by geometrical progression, until it reaches the
ninety-seventh clerk in the police-office. Now
how changed was the aspect of affairs ! A
couple of regiments of slouching Turks, preceded by the most villanous of music, tramped

over the flagstones, shattered and displaced by
recent explosions ; — lively Frenchmen were
bargaining for water-melons with blear-eyed
Tartars, or fishing for diminutive dolphin-
shaped fish with improvised fishing-tackle ;—
British sentinels were keeping guard with mea-
sured tread over dilapidated mansions, and the
shrill tones of the bagpipe echoed through deserted halls ; every house was unroofed, every
window encircled by a frame of charred wood ;
piles of rubbish blocked up the doorways ;
along the whole length of the principal street
there was scarcely a habitable mansion left—
scarcely a soul loitering under the shadow of
the ruined walls.

We toiled up the steep hill of Mithridates, and entered the museum. Here the
destruction was even more universal than
in the town, and the remains of works of ancient art, which had bravely borne the ravages
of time, lay mutilated and destroyed by the
barbarous hands of French and Turkish soldiers. Rank weeds were springing up in humid
corners, creeping along the ground, over prostrate figures, fragments of antique vases, or
blocks of marble covered with inscriptions ;

but so completely had the work of destruction been effected that I could find nothing
among the debris worth preserving.   There
was nothing left but the view ; that was always
interesting, but now how changed in its character !   We overlooked the roofless houses and
crumbling walls of the town, the sunken ships
in the bay, the grassy steppe beyond, and,
shutting in the prospect, the heights of Yenikale
crowned with the fortifications of the Allies.

Under what widely different circumstances
did I now enter almost the only entire house
which still exists, and find myself seated at
breakfast with a number of officers whom I
had last seen at a Canadian pic-nic, and in the
very room too in which I had formerly been
hospitably entertained by our late vice-consul.
Then, looking over the harbour full of shipping, our conversation was of trade ; now, we
watched a footsore regiment march down the
street on their return from a razzia, and talked
of war.

There was nothing in the present condition
of Kertch tempting enough to induce us to
prolong our stay, and I was glad to shake off
those feelings of melancholy which such scenes

as I had witnessed could not fail to produce, on board the smart little gunboat in which we ran up the Cimmerian Bosphorus to Yenikale. Here the old Tartar town, always too dilapidated to suffer very much from the most strongly developed destructive tendencies, looked very little changed from the time when I had rumbled along its single street in a Tartar waggon. There were not so many Tartars to be seen, and all the women had disappeared. There was the same variety in a military point of view which we had seen at Kertch, the same style of fortification which we had inspected at St Paul, but more substantial in its character, and the fortress seemed as well qualified to stand a siege as Sebastopol itself.

The evening found us again under way, and at daylight next morning I looked through the port-hole of my cabin upon the walls of Anapa. There was nothing very inviting in its aspect from the seaward. The fort is built upon a curved promontory, which forms an insecure bay, and which presents a precipitous cliff upwards of fifty feet in height. The fortifications, which run along the summit of this cliff, are breached here and there by the explosions of the Russian mines, which were fired by themselves before evacuating the place. To the left extends a wide plain, watered by a sluggish stream, upon which, some miles from its mouth, are situated two Cossack villages, now deserted. A range of sand-hills, covered with scrub, about five hundred feet in height, forms the background.

We were received at the little pier by a number of Circassians, whose appearance is well calculated to impress a stranger for the first time visiting their country. Their fur-caps, as tall as those of a grenadier, surmount swarthy, sun-dried, but not irregular features ; there is a fire in the eye and a compression of the lip, which marks that courage and resolution which they have so universally displayed in their prolonged contests with the Russians. Their long coats, open at the breast, reach to the knee, and are confined at the waist by a leathern girdle. A shirt covers the breast, and is closely fastened round the neck. Eight or ten bone or ivory tubes, containing powder, are ranged upon each lappet of the coat, and form the most striking feature in the costume. A plenitude of knives and pistols garnish the waist-belt. A short sword depends

from the left side, and a rifle, covered with a
sort of felt, swings at their back, and completes
their warlike accoutrements. Red or yellow
trousers are enclosed below the knee by a parti-
coloured gaiter, and a red slipper fitting closer
than the Indian moccasin, makes the most perfect *chaussure* I ever remember to have seen.
The picturesque effect of this costume is enhanced by a most independent bearing, and an
insouciance and self-confidence which suggest
that they probably understand the use of the
weapons with which they are so abundantly
supplied. When we had scrambled over a
quantity of debris through the breach in the
walls, we found ourselves in the principal street
of the place. It was, however, even in a more
ruinous condition than those we had seen at
Kertch, for the agents had been, not the be-
siegers, but the besieged. If Turks are unspar-
ing in the work of demolition, the Russians
themselves understand still better the art of
rendering every dwelling-house untenable, and
every gun unserviceable, and they can hardly
complain of the devastation caused by their
enemies, when they themselves set so brilliant
an example.

Mounted Circassians, on wiry little ponies, were galloping in every direction. Their saddles are high and narrow ; their stirrups so short, as to throw the knee almost at right angles to the horse. They seem at home only on horseback, and congregated in knots at the corners of the streets, or dismounted to ransack, in the hope of finding more spoil, some house which had already been thoroughly gutted. They watched us with no little curiosity as we walked up to a habitation which Sefer Pasha had put in decent repair, and where, seated on a high sofa smoking his chibouk, we found him holding his court. The anteroom was filled with Circassian nobles of the highest grade, who saluted us as we passed, and then crowded round the doorway to watch proceedings. These consisted in pipes, coffee, and conversation, the result of which did not give us a very favourable impression of the representative of the Sublime Porte in these regions.

Sefer Pasha is a Circassian by birth, but he has been in Turkish employ long enough to have acquired a taste for political intrigue, and the art of replenishing his purse and gratifying his private schemes of ambition at the expense of those

whom he thinks he has a right to subject to
such treatment.   The Circassians as yet are
too unsophisticated to have discovered this ;
and, carried away by religious zeal, they look
with respect and affection upon the envoy of
the Sultan.   They do not conceive it possible
that the head of their religion could be a party
to any tampering with their civil liberty ; and
until that conviction dawns upon them, Ottoman influence will be predominant.   Meantime
unscrupulous Turkish agents, dotted along the
coast, already begin to perceive that it is
their interest to depreciate Europeans, who
would not tolerate their iniquities, and to mis-
lead this ignorant people as to our real designs
with respect to their country.   They are in
consequence changing sensibly in their demean-
our towards us.   Instead of hailing us as allies
as formerly, they look with coldness and suspicion upon our advances, and protest that they
only wish to be left alone.   They say, with
some justice, that they know very little about
us.   And considering how little trouble we
have taken either to acquire information about
them, or to impart any, it is not to be wondered at if they deem us somewhat lukewarm

in the cause we pretend to have so much at heart.

Our visit to Sefer Pasha having terminated, we strolled round the fortifications of Anapa, and were struck with the pertinacity with which the Russians had destroyed everything connected with the means of defence. With one or two exceptions, the trunnions had been knocked off every gun, the platforms burnt, and here and there the fortifications levelled. We found a party of French engineers quartered here; they had been sent to blow up the fortifications upon the sea-side. Sefer Pasha had, however, objected so strongly to any demolition of what he considered the capital of his government, that he had incited the Circassians to oppose the work; and it was some months after the arrival of the French, in consequence of the strongest remonstrances, before the operation was completed.

From one point we had an extensive view over the plain, and could discern parties of mounted Circassians emerging here and there from clouds of dust, or driving cattle towards the town. The houses in Anapa are all isolated, and have been dotted about without much attempt at regularity. The hospital has been a handsome building; it is now roofless, and partly demolished. The church, however, with its green roof and belfry (from which the bell has been abstracted), is in good repair, and is converted into a Mahommedan mosque. We entered a house which had evidently been the police-office, and waded about knee-deep in Russian documents, with two or three Circassians, who seemed to take a great interest in our proceedings. We tried to learn from them a few words of their language; but the sounds were so hopeless, that, after a good deal of sneezing and coughing, as the nearest approaches we could make to them, we abandoned the attempt in despair.

I was struck with an episode which occurred while walking about the town, as being, under existing circumstances, fraught with a peculiar significance. A handsome old Circassian, followed by his squire or page, was standing looking at a collection of cannon-balls and ammunition, when a slouching Turk, who happened to be passing, but did not profess to be a sentry, told him peremptorily to move on. Upon the Circassian either not hearing or not choosing to pay attention to this command, the Turk, with a most insulting expression, threw a large fragment of wood at the page, which struck the horse. His master took the hint, and moved on without uttering a syllable of remonstrance. Had this incident occurred outside the walls, it is probable that it would have terminated in a somewhat different manner.

In the two provinces which form the northwest angle of Circassia, of one of which (Natquoitch) Anapa may be considered the capital, the old feudal system has almost disappeared, while in the provinces upon the Kuban it is still in force. The wily policy of conciliation, by wholesale bribery, pursued by Russia, resulted in the defection of many of the nobles in these two provinces, which were at the same time chiefly exposed to the depredations of her troops ; and as one by one these men temporised with Russia, they lost their hold upon the mass of the people, whose animosity against their common enemy remained in full force, and who did not derive the same advantages from an alliance with her as their more wealthy masters. The difference in the social condition of this part of Circassia from that of the in-

terior and the provinces farther east, is the
cause of one of the greatest difficulties with
which the western diplomatist has to contend.
Those influences which are in the one case
mainly to be depended upon, do not exist at
all in the other, and there is consequently an
estrangement between the tribes whose relative
position has thus become changed.

At Anapa I transferred myself to H.M.S.
" Cyclops," together with Mr Alison, who was
proceeding along the coast of Circassia upon
diplomatic service.   The " Cyclops " had been
placed at the disposal of Mr Longworth, our
civil commissioner in Circassia, whose kindness
I shall always gratefully remember, and whose
agreeable society I was fortunate enough to
share during almost the whole period of my
stay upon the coast.   I always found a home
in the " Cyclops," and have seldom been in
better quarters than in the cabin of her hospitable commander, Lieut. Ballard.

It is only a few hours' run from Anapa to
Sudjak Kaleh.   The distance by land is only
twenty-three miles.   A long promontory, while
it renders the distance considerably more by

sea, forms one shore of the deep bay, at the end of which the town is situated.

From its handsome appearance, I could hardly believe that we should find, upon landing, the same scenes of devastation ; but it was complete here as elsewhere : there were only two habitable houses left in the place. The ruins were so entirely overgrown in places, that one might have supposed many years to have elapsed since their destruction. At least a hundred mounted Circassians were collected in a shady angle of the ruined street as we approached, and greeted us in a hesitating manner, as though they were uncertain which party were the greatest intruders. They seemed to love to linger near the monuments of a power now annihilated ; and it is easy to understand the satisfaction with which they tread under foot these memorials of the former invaders of their country. With what glee they scamper on their wiry ponies down the green hill-sides which they used once to cultivate, but which have been left untouched and unfruitful for many a long year ! How merrily they journey along the sea-shore, no longer

obliged to skulk down to it between forts,
which prevented all intercourse with strangers
except at a great risk ; how they revel in their
freedom—glory in dashing along roads made
for Russian artillery, in climbing up walls over
which Russian flags once waved, and inhabiting (where they exist) houses built for Russian
soldiers ! We heard them shouting and firing
off their guns as they galloped in triumph
about the deserted squares, thus giving vent
to the exuberance of their spirits upon again
finding themselves in quiet possession of their
own property. It will be decided for them at
Paris how long they are destined to enjoy it.

Some of the chiefs whom we saw here
had just arrived from the interior, on their
way to Mustapha Pasha, at Batoum, to pay
a visit of ceremony and homage to the
representative of the Padisha in these parts.
Upon the hill to the left of the town stands a
handsome Greek church, paved with marble,
where the Russians had taken the trouble to
smash every slab. From the belfry an extensive view is obtained up the valley, from which
a small stream debouches into the harbour.
Along the banks of this stream the vegetation

is very luxuriant, but the hills which enclose
it are generally barren, covered here and there
with scrub, but nowhere attaining an elevation
of more than a thousand feet.   Over a depres-
sion in the range, a military road has been
constructed by the Russians, leading to the
Kuban.   It ascends by a succession of zigzags
up the steep side of the hills, and, winding
down the more gentle slopes to the north, extends for about forty miles to the Russian frontier.   We had intended following this road as
far as possible, and then turning to the east ;
but the jealousy of the Turks of European
influence or interference is so great, that they
succeeded in throwing obstacles in the way,
which we did not at the time think it politic
to attempt to surmount.   We therefore re-em-
barked, in time to reach Ghelendjik before
evening.   The sun was just setting as we
entered the landlocked little harbour, over-
hung by lofty hills, on which the setting
sun shed purple hues, while the white houses
of the fort contrasted strongly with the dark
green of the trees amongst which they were
buried.

Ghelendjik is about fifteen miles from

Sudjak, and, from its safe harbour, was considered by the Russians a place of some importance. There was nothing, however, to detain
us at this deserted little fort ; and so, after we
had sufficiently admired the beauty of its
position, we pursued our voyage, and found
ourselves anchored at daylight off the Russian
port of Weljaminoffsk ; or, in the Circassian
tongue, Tuapse. Here, for the first time, Circassian scenery in all its beauty burst upon us.
The hills swelled into mountains, and were
wooded to the summit, dotted with fields of
yellow corn ready for the sickle, or cultivation
of a bright green. Narrow valleys lying in
deep shade intersected the mountains, down
their sides danced sparkling streams, meeting
a little river, which, falling sluggishly into the
sea, watered a fertile plain. Upon the summit
of a hill that rose from this, appeared the white
walls of a little fort, and over them waved
lofty poplars. Behind these, a wretched regiment of Cossacks was formerly ensconced, surrounded by a hostile population. They were
completely imprisoned, and the confinement
must have been doubly irksome in the centre
of a country affording so many attractions.

We were welcomed here by a magnificent fellow, who, springing lightly from his horse, made us a respectful, but by no means servile, obeisance, and professed himself ready to do the honours of his country. Notwithstanding the native grace and dignity of his manner, he was a thorough savage, and, to one accustomed only to consider barbarians as belonging to a totally different race from ourselves, it was somewhat startling to find in the expansive forehead, the light-blue eye, and sandy hair, the transparent complexion, and exquisitely chiselled features of the Circassian chief, so perfect a type of a handsome Anglo-Saxon.

We were soon surrounded by a crowd of picturesquely attired wild-looking hill-men, all armed to the teeth, and some of them expensively dressed. They were occupying a few cottages upon the sea-shore, formerly inhabited by Russians, and told us that a good road led through the mountains in twenty hours to the Kuban. It was with some reluctance that, in spite of this intelligence, we found ourselves obliged to bid them adieu, and to leave the wondering group to watch our rapid return to the puffing monster which was to convey us

upon our southward course.   As we continued
coasting along the Circassian shore, the mountains . became higher, the scenery grander ;
every mile disclosed some new beauty, and
stimulated my desire to penetrate a country
hitherto so little known, and affording so
tempting a field for exploration.   I consoled
myself, however, by hoping that the day was
not far distant when I should be clambering
over the mountain-tops I now saw towering in
the dim distance.

CHAPTER II.

SOUCHOUM KALEH has always been considered
one of the most important places upon the
eastern coast of the Black Sea, and the Russians used to maintain here a large garrison.
Its aspect from the sea is charming ; and it
was refreshing to find, upon landing, that it
was in a better state of preservation than the
towns we had hitherto visited, and could actually boast of a resident population. The French
consul inhabited a substantial-looking mansion
upon the sea-coast. Behchit Pasha, an emascu-
lated-looking specimen of Turkish nobility, lived
in a well-built house, which had formerly belonged to some thriving Russian merchant. We
paid him a visit, and found him shivering
from the effects of fever in a confined and by
no means agreeable atmosphere. Altogether,
Souchoum was a deserted and uninviting place

at this time, so I shall reserve my description
of it for a subsequent occasion, when I visited
it with the Turkish army, and saw it under a
very different aspect.   There was one incident,
however, which occurred, worthy of notice as
forming an interesting prelude to the events
which afterwards took place.   I was standing
upon the balcony of the French consul's house,
when I was surprised by the arrival of a large
cavalcade, which came trooping up to the door
of the house in picturesque confusion.   In the
centre of the group, which was composed of
about a hundred wild-looking Circassians, rode
a handsome grey-haired man, whose tall cap
of pure white distinguished him from those by
whom he was surrounded.   There was that in
his bearing, moreover, which at once marked
him as a chief of note ; and I was not surprised to observe that, on his dismounting,
every one of his followers sprung from his
horse, and dashed at the great man's bridle,
as though vying with one another who should
be the first to render him a service.   He
received their attentions in an easy off-hand
manner, as if they were his due ; and followed
by two or three of his principal squires or

serving-men, he came up to pay us a visit. His costume was simple but handsome. A long buff-coloured coat of camel-cloth was confined round the waist by a leathern girdle, which was ornamented by a few handsomely-mounted weapons. The cartridge-tubes on his breast were of a slate-colour, and richly inlaid with silver. A pair of heavy jack-boots reached up to the thigh, and his peaked cap was trimmed with white fur. The only incongruity about the costume was a black satin stock and a shirt collar, which painfully detracted from its general effect ; indeed, when his cap was off, his jovial rubicund countenance, curly grey hair and whiskers, and well-rounded chin reposing contentedly between a pair of unmistakable gills, were precisely those of an English country gentleman. Below the neck the savage reappeared ; but the boots, though not unbecoming, were a great deal too civilised. There were no such marks of refinement about his clan. Their muscular sun-browned throats were confined by no paltry invention of modern times ; their stalwart legs were enclosed in coarse brown or yellow felt gaiters ; their well-shaped feet in red leather moccasins,——for though that is a word belonging to another hemisphere, it is the only one which in the least describes their *chaussure*. Instead of the high cap, some of these wore a species of hood similar to those of the Bedouin Arabs, the point sticking out behind, and the ends brought round the neck like a comforter. It was an agreeable variation in the costume, and added to the wildness of their aspect. About a hundred of these men filled the space in front of the house. Lounging between their horses, or squatting in groups by the roadside, they let the nags take care of themselves.

Meanwhile their lord and master, who was none other than Prince Michael—a man of some celebrity in the history of his country —discoursed with us upon the war, and the affairs of Europe generally. As he had been brought up in St Petersburg, and was a general in the Russian service, he required delicate treatment, and we dealt principally in generalities in consequence. · He little suspected that, before a month had elapsed, he would be invested by a Turkish Pasha with the office of civil governor of the province over which he had hitherto ruled by

Russian sufferance. After a long visit, a great deal of amicable chat, and the proper consumption of tobacco and coffee, our guest took his leave, and we saw him mount his fiery steed, and in the very centre of his retainers trot carelessly away along a mountain path,— the most complete instance of a feudal chieftain I had ever seen.

In the part of the Caucasus in which Prince Michael holds his sway, a new and most important element is introduced into the political condition of the country. Abkhasia, which bounds with Circassia Proper a few miles to the north of Souchoum, has an average breadth of about two days' journey, and contains a population partly Christian and partly Mahommedan. The feelings and sympathies of those entertaining such different religious sentiments are of course in every way antagonistic. Behchit Pasha and Prince Michael would not speak to one another ; the one was considered, and was, an interloper, the other looked on as a heretic ; but the Christian party attached to Prince Michael is far superior in numbers and influence to the Mahommedan party attached to Behchit.

The love of freedom, however, animates all; and the sentiments of Prince Michael with regard to Russia are certainly not participated in by his followers. On the whole, it is perhaps fortunate that the co-operation of the Abkhasians is not so important to us as that of the tribes to the north of the range. The corner of the mountains in which they live is cut off from Russia Proper by the whole of Circassia, and their assistance is not necessary to enable us to demolish the Russian army in Georgia.

It is not far from Souchoum Kaleh to the once important port of Redoute Kaleh. Soon after leaving Souchoum the high land retreats from the shore, and flat wooded plains stretch into the interior. On this account Redoute Kaleh is quite a difficult place to find on a dark night; and when morning broke, the half of the town seemed scarcely raised above the water's edge. The rising sun coloured with a vermilion tinge the snow-capped Caucasus, Mount Elbruz peering from behind a lofty range, which intercepted our view of many of the lower summits. To the south, the mountains of Gouriel and Armenia, scarcely inferior

in height, and also covered with snow, closed
the prospect ; and between these rival ranges
stretched the broad plains of Mingrelia, which
here divide Russia from Turkey, and across
which lies the road to Tiflis.

I have seldom been in a more miserable hole
than that in which two thousand five hundred
Turks had pitched their flimsy tents.   A river
with a bar at its mouth, upon which, however,
there are four or five feet of water, debouches
into the sea, and forms a sort of promontory,
upon which a few miserable wooden sheds are
built.   Between them are a number of tents, imbedded in mud ; and in the centre of the group
a large green marquee betokened the residence
of the lucky commandant, to whom we paid a
visit of condolence.   He showed us over the
camp and fortifications.   The latter consist of
earthworks, which seem to be well designed,
and which enclose the delectable assemblage
of habitations I have just described.   Outside
the fort, the tents of the soldiers extend for
some distance up the left bank of the river.
We walked up a narrow chaussé'd path, and
I never saw in the backwoods of America a
more perfect specimen of Eden than in the

swamps of Redoute Kaleh.   Many of the tents
were actually surrounded on all sides by water.
To all of them it was necessary to construct
raised causeways, plank paths, or stepping-
stones.   It seemed a perfect hotbed of fever,
and I was surprised to hear from the commandant that the troops had suffered very
slightly from illness of any kind.

A few wooden houses, which were not destroyed by the Russians, are also inhabited.
They are raised above the marsh on piles, but
the thick ooze exhales its putrid vapours through
the flooring.   The camp terminates at the junc-
tion of a river, which is connected with the
Rhion; so that Redoute Kaleh is in fact an
island raised a very little above the level of
the sea.   About eight miles distant, upon the
grassy slope of a gentle eminence, we could
discern the tents of the Russians in two lines.
They were said to number only fifty-six; but
there are probably a good many more pitched
in the wood which were not visible.   It was
scarcely possible to believe that Redoute Kaleh
was once a flourishing place, owing its importance to the fact of its having been the port of

Tiflis. A good road leads from here to that city, distant about a hundred and fifty miles.

Coasting along the low shore, we could just discern the river Rhion, which empties itself into the Black Sea by two mouths, at each of which there is a bar. Passing Skefkatil, the frontier fort of Turkey, we saw lining the water's edge, clustering upon the green hill-sides, peeping from under overhanging trees, perched upon precipitous rocks, a number of white tents, denoting, not a permanent garrison, but an army in the process of transport. It was a portion of those troops with which Omer Pasha was about to attempt to invade Georgia.

We landed under the ivy-covered battlements of the old castle of Zikinzir, from the walls of which waved the Turkish flag. The country was everywhere clothed in the richest verdure. Here and there the hill-slopes, waving with long rich grass, terminated abruptly in pre-cipitous walls of rock, to which the rank vege-tation still clung with desperate tenacity, and from which long creepers drooped into the sea. The mountains behind the castle were densely

wooded, and a lofty range of snowy peaks gave
a sterner character to scenery which combined
the most exquisite softness with features of a
sublime grandeur.   It was a fairy-like scene ;
and the delusion was scarcely dispelled when,
upon landing, we found ourselves surrounded
by swarthy Arabs, who, peering out of their
huts, looked like the slaves of some tale in the
Arabian Nights.   The officers were as black
as the men ; and a negro colonel told us
that these were Tunisian troops waiting for
the arrival of Omer Pasha.   As his Highness
had not yet arrived, we had no temptation to
linger longer at Zikinzir, though I thought it
scarcely justifiable to be contented with so
hurried a glance at such lovely scenery.   The
mountains now lined the coast all the way to
Batoum, displaying at every turn scenery of
the same character and beauty.

We had brought with us from Souchoum
Kaleh, Behchit Pasha, a perfect specimen of
the class to which he belongs.   He was
on his way to pay a visit to his superior,
Mustapha Pasha, who has been exercising,
until Omer Pasha's arrival, the supreme control in these parts.   The usual costume of

a Turkish pasha is a lavender-coloured pair of trousers—patent-leather boots—a frogged surtout, trimmed with fur—a gorgeous sword, with a scabbard mounted with gold, and belt and hilt to match—an infinity of rings upon fingers, which are ever blazing with the *tespè* —and a Fez cap. We were ushered into a room "with a fire-place at one end, and Mustapha Pasha at the other," as says *Eothen ;* and after the two great men had sufficiently kissed the hems of each other's garments, we talked in a mincing way of sublunary affairs, and were, as usual, unbounded in the expression of our mutual affection. Mustapha Pasha informed us that Omer Pasha was at Trebizond, to which place we accordingly repaired without delay. The sun was shining brightly upon its red roofs, rising one above another on the steep hill-side—upon its minarets and mosques, half hidden among waving cypresses—upon the turreted walls of its picturesque old castle, as we dropped anchor in the harbour.

The Turkish generalissimo was upon the point of embarking for Batoum, which, after mature consideration at Constantinople, had been fixed upon as his future base of opera-

tions.   Here he intended to await the arrival
of his troops.   Meantime none of these, with
the exception of a few from Bulgaria, had
made their appearance, and he entertained, in
consequence of the delay which had accompanied the departure of those from the Crimea,
but faint hopes of being able to do anything
for the relief of Kars.   He complained bitterly
of the refusal of General Pelissier to allow the
Turkish army to proceed to the seat of war in
Asia, when he first proposed an expedition
thither on the 15th of July.   It was now the
middle of September.   Sebastopol was in the
hands of the Allies ; and the Turkish army,
which had remained throughout the year in-
active in the Crimea, were still vegetating
upon that peninsula.   Only a few weeks before,
he had again made the most urgent requisition
for troops, limiting his demand to three battalions of Rifles (about two thousand strong).
Even this request was refused, and on the 6th
of September he left the Crimea for Asia, without ever having received any intimation until
he was on the point of embarking, that the
assault of Sebastopol was to take place two
days afterwards.   At this moment he was

quite unable to calculate what the numerical
strength of his army was likely to be, or when
they would be in a fit state to move.   He had
yet to learn the condition of Mustapha Pasha's
troops at Batoum, reported to be twelve thousand strong, but subsequently found to consist
of only about three hundred effective men ;
he had yet to await the arrival of fifteen thousand troops from Bulgaria, and to speculate
upon the probable period when the Allied generals in the Crimea should determine that they
could dispense with those Ottoman soldiers,
without whose protection they had not hitherto
considered the Allied armies secure, and despatch them to the relief of their countrymen
at Kars.

This event did not take place until the 29th
of September ; but as the army was almost
entirely dependent for transport on Turkish
vessels, it was with difficulty embarked by the
middle of October.   On the 26th of November,
Kars capitulated ; and although, in the opinion
of many no doubt competent to form an opinion, that city might have been relieved had
Omer Pasha landed his army at Trebizond, and
marched straight thither, it must be admitted

that to embark an army in the Crimea, to
transport it across the Black Sea ; to disem-
bark it again at the worst port upon that sea
(where it is often impossible, for a week at a
time, to communicate with the shore) ; to make
the commissariat arrangements necessary for a
large army on a long march ; to organise a land-
transport corps which could move, and therefore very different in its character from that
which, after the exertions of a year, at this
moment hampers our own army ; to march
this force for a distance of 180 miles over a
road which Curzon, Sandwith, and other travellers have described as one of the most impracticable in the world, and over two mountain-passes, at a season of the year when
they are often blocked up with snow ; and
lastly, to arrive in a condition capable of
coping with a hostile army, perfectly fresh,
and 40,000 strong,——I say that it appears
to me, that to have accomplished all this in
the short space of six weeks would have
been an achievement worthy, to say the least
of it, of a greater general than this war has
hitherto produced.

There can be no doubt, however, that had the Turkish troops in the Crimea been available some months earlier, a direct march upon Kars from Trebizond would have been practicable, if, in a military point of view, it was deemed preferable to a Georgian campaign ; but even that is in itself a very doubtful question. In the former case, nothing would have been gained beyond the raising of the siege of Kars ; in the latter, which was a far more rapid operation, the occupation of the Pass of Suramm by the Turkish army would have produced a precisely similar result, as Mouravieff must have precipitately retired to cover Gori and Tiflis, and in fact Georgia ; and in addition to this, the four Russian provinces of Imeritia, Mingrelia, Gouriel, and Abkhasia would have been in the hands of the Turks. Depôts would have been formed in Kutais, and a new base of operations established for a spring campaign. A movement of Selim Pasha's army from Erzeroum upon Akhaltzich would have secured the Turkish line of communication by the Rhion from any interruption from that quarter. It is not, therefore, difficult to perceive why, at the conference at Constantinople, a Georgian was preferred to an Anatolian campaign.

I was fortunate enough to be at Trebizond when the intelligence arrived of the fall of Sebastopol. Since the days of the Byzantine Empire this usually quiet town had never been in such a state of commotion. Sedate Turks panted breathless at the corners of the streets, with their hands pressed upon their hearts to stop the too tumultuous throb, and ejaculated "Mashallah!" Timid Greeks struck down back alleys, afraid of exciting the wrath of the conquerors ; and as they passed under our windows, we exasperated them by giving vent to our feelings of triumph. The cannon of the old castle thundered forth the news to distant villages ; the ships in the harbour were dressed out in their gayest flags ; and as evening closed in, lights began to twinkle in every balcony, and the hissing of the rockets and explosion of small-arms effectually banished sleep from the eyes of those who were disloyal enough to court it. Then revolvers and double-barrelled guns were in immense request, and a singular scene was presented in the courtyard of a hospitable merchant with whom I had been dining. Persians, Albanians, Turks, officers in the British navy, and civilians both English and French, in their different costumes, were collected under the glare of a thousand lamps, blazing away small-arms, and letting off rockets with a gusto which somewhat astonished the inhabitants of a neighbouring mansion, where the closed windows betokened that its owner was a Greek. And then with a mighty torch we paraded the streets, accompanying the national anthems, which we lustily shouted on our march, with cheers and pistol-shots. And having testified the exuberance of our joy to our hearts' content, and sufficiently astonished the Turks and frightened the Greeks, we relapsed into a softer mood, and found, ere we finished the evening, that the fairer portion of Trebizond society was not behind-hand in their manifestations of loyalty.

Like all Levantine cities, though Trebizond can scarcely be brought into that category, the society here, though small, is agreeable, and the traveller may consider himself fortunate if, in the course of his wanderings, he often stumbles

upon a place in which he may amuse himself
so well. Its scenic attractions are, moreover,
very great. The city itself is always beautiful, whether we look up at it from the sea,
or down upon it from the brow of the lofty
hill which overhangs the town ; or, riding
along its narrow streets, where overhanging
eaves shut out the sunlight, we suddenly
emerge upon one of the romantic bridges
which span the deep ravines leading to the
sea ; where the tiny rivulet at the bottom
is hidden by dense foliage, and vines and ivy
cling to lofty trees, or clamber up the precipitous sides of the ravine and overrun the
walls of the castle, perched upon its dizzy
brink ; and then following the sea-shore we
reach the commanding promontory upon which
stands the old Byzantine Church of St Sophia,
with its half-effaced frescoes and tessellated
pavement, now a Mahommedan mosque; from
here the view extends along the broken line of
coast, from whence rise lofty mountains piled
one upon the other till they reach the snow.
There is no direction in which we can go,
where there is not scenery to charm and an
object to interest. And now, as sitting upon

the veranda of our hospitable Consul, I watch the ships and steamers in the harbour, lying motionless upon its unruffled surface, my impatience to enter upon a more exciting life is not unmingled with regret, as I observe that from one of them issues a thin wreath of white smoke, which warns me that the time has arrived for me to bid adieu to the attractions of Trebizond, and steer once more for the white mountains of Circassia.

CHAPTER III.

It had been determined that on our way back
to Circassia we should again touch at Batoum
for the purpose of paying a visit to Omer
Pasha, and of observing how far the preparations for the coming campaign were advanced.
We found the green tents of the commander-
in-chief pitched upon the low promontory
which forms the eastern shore of the bay.
The miserable town had assumed quite a
bustling appearance since our last visit. The
population, indeed, was almost entirely military.
Half the shops in the filthy lane of which the
town is composed were deserted; the remainder
contained little besides vegetables, tobacco, and
Manchester calicoes. Three or four enterprising Armenian merchants had all the business
to themselves. The soldiers, who crowded
the streets in default of the ordinary popula-

tion, rejoiced in the greatest possible variety of uniform. There were Gouriel militia and Lazistan regulars, the men of Anatolia and Tunisian cohorts; Turks, European and Asiatic; Christians, infidels, and heretics. Here an English sailor would roll boisterously through the throng; there a damsel of the country shrink timidly down some side-lane, concealing her charms; while occasionally a string of peasants with laden horses wind through the swamp, their heads wrapped up after the manner of Bedouin Arabs, in cloths of different colours. Their short jackets are furnished upon each breast with ammunition-tubes; their waists are encircled with a thick shawl, in which knives and pistols are thrust; their trousers are of a thick woollen texture, loose at the hip, and fitting close at the ankles, while their feet are covered with a thick sock and sandal; a long rifle completes a costume which harmonises well with the independent bearing of the wearers; and it was some satisfaction to know that they were ready and anxious cordially to co-operate with the army whose wants they are now engaged in supplying.

I found Omer at Batoum in a state of impatient expectancy, occupied chiefly in the reorganisation of Mustapha Pasha's army, and the establishment of hospitals for them.   He told me that the accounts he had received of the country between Batoum and Kutais had induced him to change his base of operations to Souchoum Kaleh, as by so doing he would not only secure his left flank, but find a more practicable line of march.   I rode for some distance into the mountains behind Batoum, upon the road to Kutais, and certainly it was by no means of a promising character : where it is not ascending almost perpendicular hills, it is crossing swamps, in one of which my companion, Lieutenant Ballard, got bogged with his horse.

These mountains are five or six thousand feet high, and along their gloomy valleys dense mists were driving during the whole period of my stay at Batoum.   Souchoum was the only other port upon the coast, as the roadstead of Redoute Kaleh was not considered sufficiently safe to land the army.   Moreover, the road to the interior from thence passes between an impracticable swamp on the one hand, and the river Chopiscal on the other, and was reported (as we afterwards found truly) to be occupied by several lines of defences, which could not be turned.   There is no road from Batoum to Kars direct.

The arrangements of the commander-in-chief were a good deal disconcerted by the deplorable condition in which he found the army of Mustapha Pasha, which had been quartered here.   These troops, which had numbered twelve thousand strong, now only mustered three hundred effective bayonets.   Mustapha Pasha had been despatched by Omer to Constantinople to answer for his misdeeds.   As soon as these had been clearly and indisputably proved against him, he was sent back by his government to his old post, and placed at the head of an even larger force than that which he had originally commanded, for the purpose of co-operating with Omer Pasha upon the left bank of the Rhion, which he did by marching ten miles into Gouriel and back again, having been two months engaged in effecting the important operation.

Meanwhile transports loaded with material for the army began daily to arrive, and nothing could exceed the energy and good

management with which the transport-service
was carried on.   The entire provisioning of the
troops, the land-transport animals, and almost
the whole of their transport across the sea, was
accomplished by Turkish means.   And when
it is considered that within a month from this
period the army was in a condition to move
into the interior, it must be admitted that no
time was lost at the outset.

There was not much to tempt us to remain
at Batoum, so we returned to Souchoum, touching on the way at some places on the coast.
About ten miles to the north of Batoum is
Shefkatil, formerly the frontier port of Turkey
in this direction.

We landed here, and found a garrison of
about six hundred Turkish soldiers, who occupied a small hillock, encircled on three sides by
a swamp, and on the fourth by the Tchorock.
The wooden houses in the fort are perfectly
riddled by round shot, thrown in by the Russian fleet at the commencement of the war.

The fort upon the north side was defended
by Colonel Yordan, to whose gallantry the
salvation of the place is due.   When the
Russian fleet first anchored off the mouth of

the river, they opened their fire upon the fort upon the south side, commanded by a Turk, who replied to it but feebly. The northern forts, however, returned so brisk a cannonade that the ships turned their attack entirely upon Yordan, who, after a sharp conflict, in which the Turkish commander did not join, succeeded in beating them off. When the affair was over, and Yordan indignantly demanded of his colleague the reason of the silence of his batteries, he replied, naively enough, " Why should I fire ? They did not fire upon me." The walls of the room in which I was regaled with pipes and coffee, were pierced in six places.

I found it difficult to recognise Souchoum under the different aspect in which I now again beheld it. The sequestered harbour, upon which not even a Turkish boat was formerly anchored, was now crowded with shipping ; its silent streets and deserted shops were now inhabited by a bustling population. From sunrise to sunset it was the scene of unwearied activity. Troops were continually arriving in steamers, and being landed without a moment's delay; and it seldom happened that one of these vessels remained more than twenty-four hours

in port.   The troops which had already arrived
were principally those from Bulgaria, while the
Rifles from the Crimea, under Colonel Ballard,
at last made their appearance.   The men were
well supplied with provisions, and were principally encamped upon the hill behind the town,
so as to be removed from the influence of the
marsh malaria.   Thousands of horses and cattle
grazed upon the rich pasture of the plains, destined to share their duties as beasts of burden
with the hardy Bulgarian peasants, who have
been imported from Varna for that purpose.
Their services were especially valuable, as so
much of the camp was situated upon the top
of the short but steep hill.   The houses were
very substantial, and have suffered but little
from the change of circumstances under which
they were now occupied.

Souchoum is one of the places upon the
coast which were not destroyed by the Russians prior to their evacuation.   The work
of demolition, therefore, having been left to
the Turks, is not nearly so entire.   There
is a good street running along the shore,
where the shops were being gradually opened
by speculators who follow the army.   At one

end of the street is a square old Turkish fort, built in the year 1578, with a crenellated wall, and containing cannons, poplars, the tombs of sundry pashas and princes of the country, and dilapidated barracks ; at the other was the handsome two-storeyed house afterwards occupied by Omer Pasha, and some of the large buildings which were formerly the club and casino, government offices, &c., &c. At right angles to this street is an avenue, about a quarter of a mile long, leading to the hill upon which the Russian hospitals were formerly situated. From here I used to watch troops disembarking, collecting on the quay, pitching their tents, or going through their drill. The plains were covered with people and cattle, and as a party of wild Abkhasians come galloping in from the mountains on their wiry ponies, they pull up with astonishment upon the brow of the hill, and gaze wonderingly at the scene below; for they see the plain that was so solitary, and the town that was deserted a month ago, now alive with an active population; and as they listen to the roll of the drums, or watch the glitter of the bayonets in the sunshine, they perceive in them the indications of

the change which seems about to take place in
the destinies of their country.

Scarcely a century had elapsed since Otho-
man troops such as these had been quartered
in the old castle on the sea-shore, where then,
as now, upon the plain at their feet, lived a
Mussulman population.   They had themselves
assisted in ridding their country of these invaders only to make way for the soldiers of
the Czar, who had, in their turn, been now
compelled to relinquish their stronghold in
Abkhasia to their old enemies.   Thus did the
natural possessors of the soil witness, from the
mountain-tops, foreigners fighting for their fertile valleys, and find themselves the victims of
a quarrel between the two most barbarous nations in Europe, the object of whose strife
each alleges to be the advance of civilisation
and the general wellbeing of society.

A little after sunrise on the morning of the
3d of October a salute, of nineteen guns, thundered forth by the Turkish men-of-war lying
in the harbour, informed the Turkish army encamped at Souchoum Kaleh that their commander-in-chief had arrived.   It was the signal
for universal bustle and activity, and in less

than half-an-hour the shore was alive with troops. Infantry, artillery, and cavalry extended themselves in a long line upon the coast, prepared to submit to the scrutinising gaze of the general. As Omer Pasha left the " Cyclops," which had gone back to bring him, the ship manned yards; the merchant vessels were decked out in their gayest flags; the music of regimental bands came across the water, and as he landed he was saluted by the guns of a tabia scarcely yet completed. His Highness, accompanied by his staff, at once proceeded to inspect his troops; and although the force as yet collected was not very large, he had every reason to be satisfied with the condition in which he found it. His exertions at Batoum had been ably seconded by Ferhad Pasha the chef-d'etat-major, and Achmet Pasha the admiral. The miserable army of Mustapha Pasha could scarcely recognise itself; the healthy were undergoing their regular discipline, the number of convalescents was rapidly increasing, and the sick found themselves, to their astonishment, in hospital. It did not seem to have occurred to Mustapha Pasha that such an establishment was a neces-

D

sary appendage to an army. News to the effect that the troops in the Crimea were embarking in good earnest, and might soon be expected, put us all into good spirits, and I began to think, after all, that although we could not actually relieve Kars, we might yet deprive Russia of such an amount of territory as might be deemed an equivalent to it.

Meantime there was some political work to be done. Prince Michael, who, under the Russian regime, exercised the chief power in Abkhasia, found himself in an extremely difficult position, and had no alternative but to adopt a conciliatory policy. At the same time, as his sympathies were decidedly Russian, and as, in the opinion of Omer Pasha, he was not altogether to be depended upon, he determined to commit him thoroughly by appointing him civil governor of Souchoum. The ceremony took place with great state; the road was lined with troops from Prince Michael's house to that of Omer Pasha; the captains of the English and French men-of-war, the English and French commissioners, and everybody of importance in the place, were present in full dress. The room was also filled with the principal chiefs of the surrounding country, and some of those from

PRINCE MICHAEL OF ABKHASIA (HAMID BEY.)

civilities in

in his room. A most distant

center of the English

whose military remained in West

A good many received us

about this time places of Christ

of my children we returned

after weeks previously

interesting features in the

of wisdom but it was difficult to

them information with respect

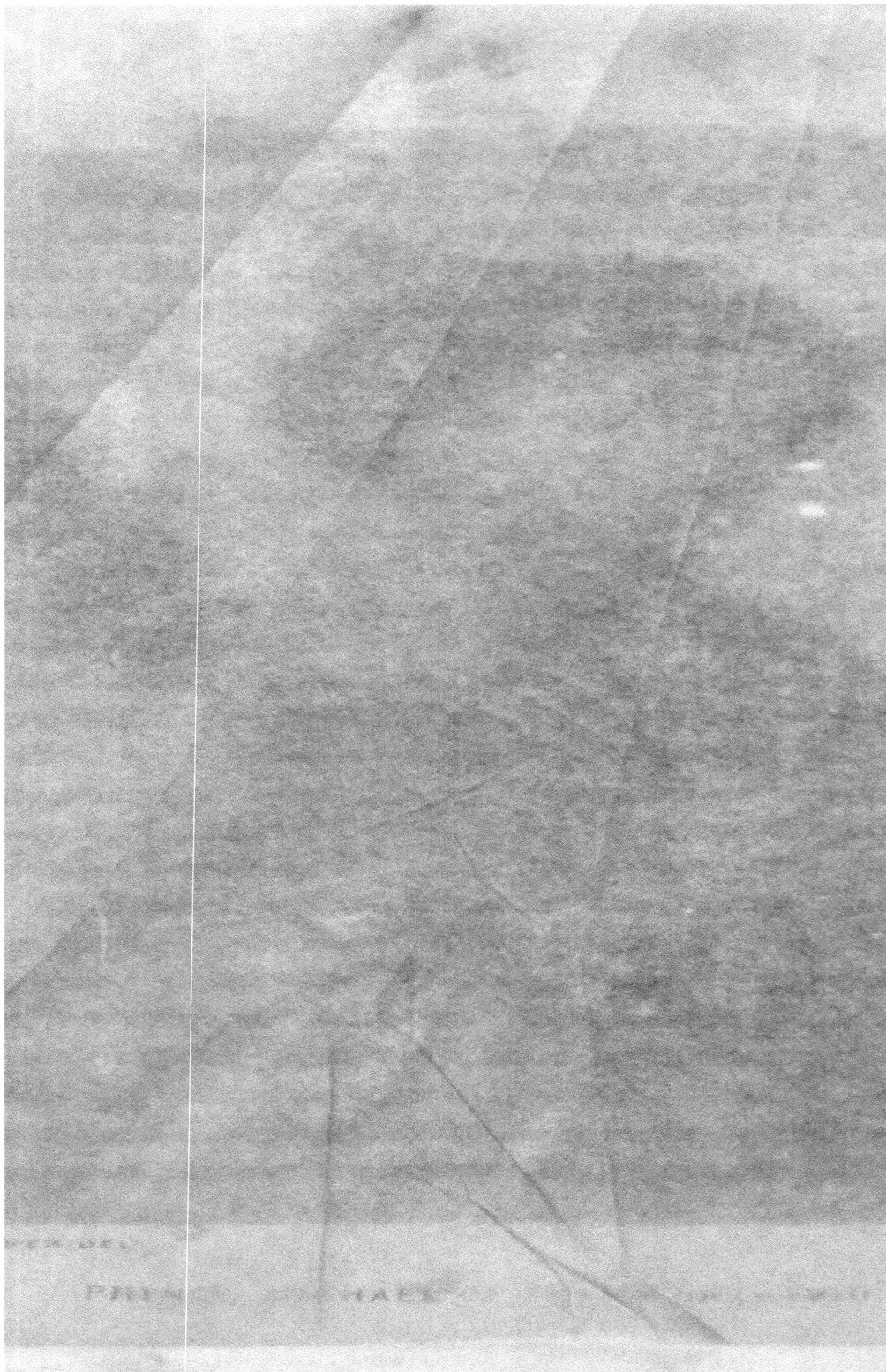

distant tribes were present. The group was in the highest degree striking and picturesque. Prince Michael himself was in full Abkhasian costume, but evidently little expected the grand public display, the object of which was to give as much importance and publicity as possible to his acceptance of authority from the Porte. While a salute was being fired, Omer Pasha proclaimed him governor of the town, and, turning to the chiefs present, said : " You have always acknowledged the authority of Hamid Bey (Prince Michael); all I ask of you now is, to continue to regard him in the same light as you have hitherto done." Everybody seemed immensely pleased except Hamid Bey, who looked rather as if he suspected that he was being taken in; but after a fresh interchange of civilities, he was marched off to his abode. Prince Michael is married to the sister of the Princess Dadian, whose authority is paramount in Mingrelia.

A good many Circassians arrived at Souchoum about this time at the behest of Omer, who had caused proclamations to be issued requiring their attendance some weeks previously. These formed an interesting feature in the population of the place; but it was difficult to gain from them any information with respect to the interior, partly because few of them speak Turkish, and partly because those who did were somewhat suspicious of strange interrogators, and under any circumstances preferred to impart false to true information.   The story of the Cadi of Karachai, who had just arrived from his mountain province lying on the northern slopes of Mount Elbruz, was therefore to be taken with a reservation, nothwithstanding that the author was a chief-justice.   He reported that the Naib had made a descent upon Karachai with fifteen hundred men, and had informed the inhabitants of the province that they were to join him at once in an attack upon the Russians.   They represented to the Naib the inexpediency of such an expedition in the face of the Russian force to which they were opposed, and the difficulties they would encounter; but upon his insisting on carrying out his project, they absolutely refused, and the Naib found to his dismay that most of the nobles were in the Russian interest, and that he could expect no assistance from this quarter, in which Russia was paramount, so he was obliged to return to Abbasack.   The Naib, not long afterwards, made his appearance at Souchoum to tell his own story.

The country in the neighbourhood of Souchoum is so singularly beautiful, and unlike
any other part of the world, that I was never
tired of exploring its wooded valleys, or scrambling on a Circassian pony to the summits of
the hills, which command magnificent views
in every direction. I found that Omer was no
less fond of making voyages of discovery than
myself, and he never lost an opportunity
of becoming personally acquainted with the
country in the immediate neighbourhood of
his camp. Upon one of these occasions, Mr
Longworth and I accompanied him for some
distance into the interior. After having inspected the hospitals, and the fortifications
which were being erected to the rear of the
hill, and galloped over the mountain-slopes
covered with fern, in search of the most eli-
gible site for the camp of the battalions still
expected, his Highness struck right into the
mountains by a narrow path, along which we
followed our Abkhasian guides for about two
hours. The path led through a narrow gorge;
the sides of the lofty hills which enclosed it
were clothed with pendulous forests. So narrow was the valley, and so magnificent the timber, that we seemed almost buried in foliage;

wild grapes clambered over the loftiest trees, and hung above us in tempting festoons; gigantic fig-trees spread out their fantastic branches loaded with wild but luscious fruit; apples, pears, and walnuts, all of a fair quality, were to be had for the trouble of stretching out the hand; but the rapidity with which his Highness got over the ground, removed all danger of our making ourselves ill from any such indulgence.

We splashed along, followed by fifty or sixty mounted orderlies, through mud and jungle, until we emerged upon an open space on which a village was situated, when the women and children rushed frightened and crying into their konaks, and the men collected round the doors not a little bewildered and astonished at so unusual an apparition. However, they soon regained confidence, and came to kiss the skirts of Omer Pasha's coat, and offer us hospitality. We therefore dismounted at the door of the principal cottage in the village—the only one constructed of planks—and made ourselves comfortable. Omer Pasha, who is eminently gallant, knocked at the door of a room into which a bevy of fair damsels had bolted themselves, and told them there was nothing to be afraid of. He was obliged to exercise his powers of persuasion for some time before he could induce them to open a chink large enough for us to see the sparkle of their eyes. However, they gradually relented, and before we left, their shyness had quite disappeared. They spun, embroidered, and netted for our edification, and we were much struck by the ingenuity they manifested in their female accomplishments. One or two of the girls were remarkably pretty, differing neither in complexion nor in the character of their features from those in our own country. Their hands and feet, which were bare, were very small and delicate. Their costume is by no means so picturesque as that of the men : it consisted simply of a sort of loose dressing-gown open at the bosom, and confined by a girdle at the waist. Most of the houses are constructed of " wattle and dab," and thatched with the stalks of Indian corn.

Meantime the male portion of the community had not been idle, and we found a breakfast of youghourt (sour milk), honey, pasta (Indian-corn bread), and pumpkin, by no means unacceptable after our ride. Omer Pasha made presents to the ladies, patted and praised the children, said civil things to the men, and behaved very much as if he was

soliciting the suffrages of the population at
the next general election.   Then we mounted
our horses, and galloped back again.   On our
way we were overtaken by some of our late
entertainers, who breathlessly informed us that
a slave had taken advantage of the commotion
which our visit to the village had caused to
make his escape.   We had not proceeded half
a mile before a ragged figure came bounding
out of the thicket like a startled deer, and
threw himself at Omer Pasha's feet.   He was
a Circassian boy of about eighteen, who two
months before had been kidnapped by the Abkhasians, and had thus contrived to fly from his
present owners.   His Highness did not hesitate
an instant to assure him of his freedom ; and
although by so doing he must have in some
degree alienated the goodwill of the people of
the country, he said, in discussing the policy of
the act afterwards, that he felt it was a duty
which his feelings of humanity, whatever might
be its political consequences, imposed upon him,
and that he was determined, under all circumstances, to do his utmost to put a stop to the
system of man-stealing and slavery which at
present exists among the tribes of the Caucasus.   These professions, however, were not

altogether borne out by his subsequent conduct. For the rest of the way our ragged
attendant kept up with us with a light heart
and as light a foot. He seemed never to think
himself safe unless he was almost ridden over
by the guard. I afterwards saw this boy again
in the full enjoyment of his liberty in his
native village among the mountains of Circassia.

CHAPTER IV.

DURING my stay at Souchoum I was hospitably entertained by Mons. Champoiseau, the French consul, whose balcony, overlooking the harbour, was the most interesting post of observation. At last, however, I got tired of looking at steamers towing transports in and out ; at horses jumping overboard and swimming ashore ; at soldiers squatted in groups upon the quay, with their arms piled before them, munching biscuits, or fabricating cigarettes. The discordant notes of their eversounding bugles distracted me. Shooting at gulls with a revolver was an amusement which had at length lost its charm, and even riding through the magnificent country was becoming less interesting, now that we had pushed our explorations in every direction as far as it was prudent to venture. So we determined to make an expedition, as far as it was practicable, along the future line of our march upon Sugdidi, and afterwards to reconnoitre the fort of Anaklea from the sea. Our party consisted of Mr Longworth, the English civil commissioner, and his secretary; MM. Champoiseau and de Vilmorin; and Colonel Ballard, an English officer attached to the Turkish army, and who has followed its fortunes ever since the memorable siege of Silistria, where he remained, after the death of Butler and the departure of Nasmyth, to share in the triumphant results of that gallant defence, and witness the retreat of the Muscovite legions.

In consequence of the delays attendant upon all movements in the East, we did not start until the afternoon of the 7th of October, and even then, in despair at the non-appearance of our guides, rashly determined to find our way to Shemsherrai without them.

The sandy road by which we left Souchoum skirted the shores of its beautiful deep bay, where wooded hills come down to the water's edge, and deep glens wind into the Caucasian chain, affording us occasional glimpses of glaciers and icy peaks : of these the Djoumantau, which attains an elevation of upwards of 12,000 feet, is the most prominent. Passing the old Greek church of Okhvamè, whose ruined walls are almost hidden amid a mass of rich foliage, we reach the picturesque habitation of Hassan Bey, an uncle of Prince Michael's, whose old feud with his relative can scarcely yet be said to be extinct, and who, though by no means a friend of the Russians, has prudently kept out of the way. His house commands an enchanting view of the rich valley of the Kelassur, now a harmless stream, but with a broad stony bed denoting its winter character. Along the hill on the opposite side we observe the remains of the old wall, which was built, some centuries before Christ, by the Greeks, to defend the flourishing colonies which they had founded upon the delta of the Kodor, from the warlike Koraxiens who inhabited the mountains in their rear.

The road passes near the old tower which terminated the wall at this point, from which, according to Dubois de Montpereux, it extended in a semicircular direction for about eighty miles to Anaklea. It is singular that, like the old Greek wall which, running from Balaklava to Inkermann, enclosed the peninsula upon which Sevastopol was afterwards built, this wall should, at a remote period, have enclosed a fort of the same name ; for when Dioscurias, the principal colony within its circumference, and the emporium of commerce upon this coast, was conquered by Mithridates, upon its site was built the castle of Sevastopol. It was burnt by the Romans when the Persians, under Chosroës, afterwards threatened to attack it, and subsequently rebuilt under its old name of Sevastopolis by Justinian. For some time afterwards, the country through which we were now journeying was a flourishing province. A large Christian population owned spiritual allegiance to a bishop, whose residence was at Drandy, the village at which we hoped to pass the night ; but when at last the kings of Georgia ceased to rule over Abkhasia, its prosperity waned, and it ultimately became the neglected and thinly-populated district which we now found it.

Leaving the Kelassur, where the attractions of beautiful scenery are so much enhanced

by interesting associations, we followed a
track which diverged from the sea-coast, and
for hours pursued our way through a dense
and magnificent forest. Gradually the path
became less distinct, muddy ravines impeded
our progress, and we were often puzzled to
cross the treacherous swamps, in which we were
by no means desirous of leaving our horses.
Meantime we had got separated from our servants and baggage, the night was closing in, and
we found our position becoming momentarily
more disagreeable. One of the party climbed
to the top of the highest tree, in a vague hope
of seeing the sea ; but he reported that nothing
was visible but a boundless expanse of tree
tops, so we pushed wearily on till the sound of
chopping fell pleasantly upon our ears; and we
came upon a small clearing just in time to see
two wild men of the woods take to their heels,
and scramble with the utmost nimbleness to
the top of a tree. Never in their lives before,
probably, had they seen the apparition of such
a party, and it was some time before we could
assure them of our harmless character—a task
rendered doubly difficult by our utter ignorance

of their language, and the impossibility of communicating with them except by signs.

At last a boy slowly descended, and upon our naming the village of Drandy, which we intended to make our night-quarters, volunteered to conduct us thither. We soon after emerged upon an open space, where a few cottages were surrounded by some fields of Indian corn, the whole shut in by hills clothed with magnificent timber. Here we created an immense sensation; the dogs assailed us furiously, the women flew from house to house, evidently with the intention of barricading themselves in and standing a siege; while the men collected in a formidable group, and favoured us with a stare which did not tend to reassure us.

They stoutly denied that their village was called Drandy, and expected that we were to be satisfied with this assurance, and dive into the woods again. This was a prospect which, at 6 o'clock P.M., was not to be entertained for an instant, so we intimated to them that if they did not give us a guide to show us the real Drandy, we should assume that it was a " Mrs

Harris," and in default of a formal invitation, quarter ourselves where we then were. Upon this decision becoming apparent, one of the party volunteered to lead us. In fact, it was quite evident that our visit was extremely unpalatable, so we were not sorry to leave so inhospitable a spot, and tempt our fate once more. Our guide was an independent, cynical-looking fellow, who, after getting us well into the wood, expressed his determination to leave us there. On our objecting to this, he jumped up on my pony behind me without the slightest notice, and, affectionately embracing me round the waist, told me to lead the way. In this manner we scrambled on, until I found the hands gradually relaxing their hold, a circumstance which warned me to be ready to seize my friend by the collar, which I did, when a moment afterwards he slipped nimbly off and tried to make his escape. It now became necessary to point out to him in a friendly way the use and merits of a revolver, with which he was so much impressed that he got tamely up again, and I took a turn of his coat round my arm as a precautionary measure : so finding escape impos-

sible, he consoled himself by emptying my car-
tridge-pouch of its contents, and transferring
them to his own pockets, as I discovered on
the following day.

It was dark when we once more quitted
the forest and entered the village of Drandy,
to meet, alas! with a similar reception to
the one we had already experienced. Observing the temper of the population, we commenced proceedings by taking possession of
an unoccupied house, after which it became
necessary to make some attempts at conciliation, preparatory to getting something for dinner. Gradually confidence was restored, and
after we had kissed the babies, flattered the
mammas, and presented the papas with irresist-
ible sixpences fresh from the mint, there remained only the old women to vanquish ; but
they were inexorable. They stormed and
railed at our impertinent intrusion, and would
not be appeased by the most insinuating de-
meanour. To the last they insisted that we
were Russians (indeed, this opinion was pretty
general), and protested against any hospitality
being shown to us. However, the shining six-

pences carried the day, and cocks and hens with their throats cut were soon strewn around us in a profusion refreshing to behold. Then came honey and milk, Indian-corn bread, curds, and eggs; so we soon consoled ourselves for the misfortunes of the day, and even thought slightingly of our servants and baggage, who, overtaken by the night, were straying somewhere in the woods up to their knees in mud.

After dinner I visited a cottage with de Vilmorin, where a charming young mother was nursing a baby, and the handsome father, who had taken a fancy to us from the beginning, invited us to sit down. Presently two or three young ladies dropped in, then some village gallants; and a half-witted youth came and played upon a rudely-constructed lyre, from which he drew wild but not unmusical sounds; so we assisted in culinary operations, and sketched the ladies, and exchanged pipes with the gentlemen, and explained that we were "Anglia" and "Frances," a fact which excited their curiosity as much as our assurance that we were Christians did their astonishment. When we made the sign of the cross their satisfaction was complete, and we spent a most pleasant evening, until we were interrupted by the arrival of our baggage, and our little-expected blankets were doubly welcome as we coiled ourselves upon the hard boards round the fire, and floundered, in our dreams, through the mud.

Cart of the Country.

CHAPTER V.

WE were up at daybreak next morning, and having procured a guide, were soon *en route*. From the brow of the hill overhanging the Kodor we could just discern the sea. Here was situated the picturesque ruin of the old cathedral, whose crumbling walls evidenced the decay of the province since the days in which Drandy had been a bishop's see.

The Kodor is the largest stream in Abkhasia, and near its mouth had been situated the old Greek colony of Dioscurias. It was not without some difficulty that we succeeded in finding a ford. The country through which we passed was richly wooded, but not thickly inhabited. The villages were always in the centre of a few acres of cultivation, and the handsome trees, standing singly in the Indian-corn fields, were covered with vines. The natives press their wine in a hollow tree like a canoe, across the centre of which is a strainer. The canoe is slightly tilted, and the grapes are pressed in the upper end. We saw the peasants loading their strange wicker-work carts with the rich clusters that hung overhead. These carts are oblong baskets, eighteen or twenty feet long, and four or five wide. The wheels are solid, and placed very far back—the fore part of the basket resting upon the pole, and projecting between the buffaloes as far as their shoulders. The houses are almost universally made of wattle, and thatched with Indian corn. In most of the villages there are both Christian and Mussulman inhabitants; but none of the women cover their faces, or are more shy than savages generally. Their dress appears, to a stranger's eye, identical with that of the Circassians; but the natives detect at a glance the nationality of the wearer, partly from a slight difference in the arms, and partly from the cut of the coat, the skirt of which in the Abkhasians is formed of a greater number of pieces "let in" than in those of the Circassians. The men all carry a gun slung at their backs. They are naturally afraid of committing themselves by

E

hospitality to strangers in time of war, while, at the same time, they profess sympathy with any invaders whose object is Russian expulsion.

In the afternoon we again struck the Russian road from which we had strayed the day before, and shortly after reached Shemsherrai, the first important place upon the line of march, about thirty-six miles from Souchoum, and situated upon the sea, three miles from the point at which the road strikes into the interior. We found that it was not safe to proceed by land beyond this point. A Russian force of four thousand men was stationed at Sugdidi, thirty-two miles distant, and the intermediate country was completely in the hands of the Russians, and occupied by Mingrelian militia. We heard here that a number of Cossacks and militia were at Anaklea, and it was important to discover the truth of the rumour ; we therefore embarked on board the "Cyclops" and "La Vigie," which met us here, and proceeded to the mouth of the Ingour.

Fort Anaklea is a picturesque ruin, situated upon the left bank of the river, and surrounded by a dense forest. As we saw smoke rising from behind the fort, it was judged necessary to enter the river with an armed force in case of an ambuscade. Seven boats, with a force of about seventy men, under Lieutenant Ballard of the " Cyclops," and Lieutenant de Vilmorin of " La Vigie," pulled towards the mouth of the river, which was completely commanded by the guns of the vessels. We found five feet of water upon the bar of the Ingour, which is one of the most considerable streams upon this coast. Upon our landing at the fort, we came upon the smoking embers of a fire, which our guide told us was that of the militia : a perfect stillness, however, prevailed everywhere —not a human being seemed in the neighbourhood ; and the wood was so thick that we did not anticipate much warning from the men stationed in the maintop of the "Cyclops" to give an alarm. We proceeded up the bank of the river for some time, and came upon the ruins of the village of Anaklea, of which a few charred logs alone remain. Having satisfied our curiosity, we were returning to the boats, when two musket-shots from the " Cyclops" threw our party into a state of some excitement. We immediately threw out skirmishers to protect our embarkation, and soon after saw a large group of persons collected at some distance up the river. As they seemed to be people of the country, Messrs Longworth and Champoiseau went up with a flag of truce, with M. de Vilmorin, our guide, and myself.

One of the group, putting his white cap upon the top of his gun, by way of responding to our flag, came forward to meet the interpreter, and we learned from him that the immediate neighbourhood of Anaklea was comparatively free of Russians, that the nearest large force lay at a distance of nine miles off, and that they rarely visited Anaklea. The people professed themselves in the highest degree friendly, and we gave them a sovereign to cement the alliance. From the accounts of these men, the whole Russian force within a circuit of fifteen miles from Anaklea amounted to ten thousand men. The most important point, and the one at which the first struggle was to be anticipated, was at the fortress of Roukh, upon the Ingour, about six miles from Sugdidi.

Taking "La Vigie" in tow, we returned to Shemsherrai the same evening. It is a considerable place; at present only partly inhabited. The Greek and Russian population have shut up their shops and decamped, and the Turkish merchants have it all their own way. Prince Michael has a handsome house here, built of wood in the Russian style. It is his principal residence. At a distance of three hours are his game-preserves, where he strictly prohibits any one from poaching his wild boar, wild sheep, and deer.

The limits of Prince Michael's jurisdiction in this direction are not clearly defined. He claims Samursachan, a province lying between Abkhasia and Mingrelia, on the frontier of which Shemsherrai is situated, and the people of Anaklea professed to owe him allegiance, but it is very certain that his powers of protection do not extend beyond Shemsherrai. As we rode out of the town, on our way back to Souchoum, we found that there was an addition to our party, who announced himself to be a Pole, the slave of a Turk in Shemsherrai. He spoke to one of our servants, who was also a Pole, and informed him that he and six of his unfortunate compatriots were at that moment slaves to Turks in Shemsherrai. We assured him that his freedom would be obtained, but insisted upon his returning; for the masters of the other slaves, finding we had liberated one, would have secreted the others : they were thus thrown completely off their guard, and Omer Pasha afterwards assured me of his intention to liberate them.

The Russian road by which we now journeyed generally follows the sea-coast, crossing the mouths of innumerable rivers, the bridges over which were almost invariably destroyed. We slept at a large village upon the other side of the Kodor, in a magnificent situation ; the lofty elm-trees being completely hidden by masses of wild vine. Here we were hospitably received ; a comfortable hut was placed at our disposal, soft coverlets and pillows were arranged upon wooden stretchers, and we passed a most civilised night. The staple food of the country is pasta, or Indian-corn bread, almost exactly similar to that of the United States, and quite as good. The cheese is eatable, but very salt, and boiled pumpkin is popular ; fruit is abundant : so that, for a wild country, the living is upon the whole above the average.

When we were within a few miles of Souchoum we met three squadrons of cavalry, the *avant garde* of the army which was moving into Mingrelia; our information about the road was therefore very acceptable, and I was quite astonished at the rapidity with which Omer Pasha was hurrying on his campaign. Troops were disembarking with unusual rapidity; the "Great Britain" disgorged eighteen hundred men in an incredibly short time, and returned for more. There had been twenty thousand men landed within a fortnight. The Duke of Newcastle had also arrived in the "Highflyer," from Anapa and Sudjak. On her way the "Highflyer" picked up the Naib, who was coming to pay Omer Pasha a visit. He declared his expedition against the Russians to have been eminently successful, which was somewhat at variance with the report of the Karachai men, to which I have already alluded. At all events, Omer Pasha evidently had a high opinion of his power and influence in the country, as he appointed him Civil Governor of all the provinces of Circassia, from the country of Schamyl to the provinces of Tchapsugh and Natquoitch, which are at present under the jurisdiction of Sefer Pasha. The terms of his "bouyourouldi" were almost identical with those of Prince Michael ; the object of the appointment was in both cases the same.

On the following morning our slumbers were disturbed by the thunder of cannon, and we saw the ships in the harbour decked out with flags. We found the cause of these rejoicings to be the arrival of despatches from Kars, announcing the glorious repulse of the Russian army. Looking out of my window, I saw Omer Pasha informing his army of the fact, which they received with loud cheers. It was an inspiriting sight, after having exhorted his soldiers to march to the entire annihilation of the army which their comrades had almost destroyed, to see his Highness, upon a prancing charger, lead his battalions to the war. Five thousand men, with two batteries of artillery, followed him along the Kutais road. The moment was well chosen, and the music of their bands harmonised well with the booming of the heavy guns, which were still celebrating the victory. The troops were in good heart, and had perfect confidence in their General, and in the successful issue of the campaign in which they were engaged.

As a considerable portion of the army was

still to arrive, and the preparations for their departure, together with the march to Shemsherrai, would necessarily occupy some time, and it was not to be expected that Omer Pasha would be in presence of the enemy for at least a month, I gladly availed myself of the kind invitation of the Duke of Newcastle to accompany him upon a trip into the interior, from which I returned just in time to join the main body of the army on its march from Shemsherrai. As, however, the incidents of that expedition are in no way connected with the campaign, it is not necessary to trouble the reader with an account of them at present. But I must not avail myself of this excuse, to omit mentioning a *chasse* to which Prince Michael invited the Duke of Newcastle, Mr Calthorpe, and myself, at his game-preserves, about fifteen miles distant from Shemsherrai. We rode thither, accompanied by about one hundred of the Prince's followers, and made quite a picturesque procession. His shooting-box was a little wooden habitation, in the midst of a dense forest of the most gigantic trees I have ever seen in any part of the world. Here he made us very comfortable, and gave us

some delicious Russian tea. Indeed, all the
evidences of civilisation by which we were
surrounded were Russian, and the Prince himself seemed by no means happy under his new
allegiance. It is to be hoped that his unfortunate Highness will not ultimately be sent to
Siberia as a penalty for having had Turkish
honours forcibly thrust upon him.

We strolled through some covers in the afternoon, and a deer which we saw, besides numerous
traces of wild boar, gave us hope for the organised hunt of the morrow. When, however, on
the following morning, I saw the character of
the dogs and the limited number of beaters, I
confess that these were considerably damped,
and the subsequent arrangements did not show
that our host was a very artistic sportsman.
The hunting-ground was a large plain, separated from the sea by a belt of the forest,
which surrounded it in every other direction ;
the cover consisted of high fern, with clumps
of birch and alder, through which it was
with the utmost difficulty that the beaters
forced their way : we were placed upon the
side of this cover, and it was so thick that the
animals passed through it without our per-

ceiving them. The Duke made a splendid shot at a deer, as he showed himself for an instant at a distance of upwards of a hundred yards, bounding through the fern. From the excitement which this success caused — the triumph of the Prince, and the perfect satisfaction depicted upon the countenances of his followers—I suspected that the Prince's sport usually consisted simply in shooting *at* his game. Neither Calthorpe nor I were lucky enough to have an opportunity of doing even this ; but we were shortly afterwards joined by Captain Moore and some of the officers of the "Highflyer" (which was anchored upon the coast), and we soon heard a fusillade of a dozen shots, characteristic of the sanguine temperament of the naval brigade. These gentlemen had at once stumbled upon a pig, who had apparently amused himself by dodging between their legs, and was reported to have received twelve balls in his head, at a distance of about ten yards. Notwithstanding this excellent practice, the porker was nowhere to be discovered ; but rather than entertain for a moment the unworthy suspicion that he had been missed, we consoled our friends by reminding them that

Russian pigs could stand a deal more pounding than Russian sailors. We were now a large party, with a scanty supply of horses, so we rode double down to the sea-beach, the soft mud through which we boldly galloped giving us confidence ; and it was with a strange feeling of desolation that I saw the middy, who had been so tenderly clasping me, jump into his boat ; and, bidding adieu to his hospitable captain, in whose ship I had so often found a cordial welcome, and to those in whose interesting companionship I had scrambled over the mountains of Circassia, watched their receding boats, and found myself the only representative of my nation amongst that wild group of Abkhasians.

CHAPTER VI.

THERE was no little preparation necessary for an expedition *en amateur* with the Turkish army. Having, however, bought the necessary horses, and been furnished by Omer Pasha with rations and a tent, I found myself on the 30th October pushing on with the utmost expedition for the *avant poste* of the army, which was encamped within three hours' march of the Ingour. Mr Longworth had also determined to follow the army, and was now waiting to start with Omer Pasha and the main body. At about seven miles from Shemsherrai the road crosses the Godova river, and finally leaves the coast. The country is flat, but for the most part covered with a dense forest, where swamps frequently occur which are calculated seriously to impede the progress of an army on the march. I found myself surrounded by a miscellaneous concourse, straggling by devious paths through the tangled underwood, or ploughing their way through the deep mud. There were infantry and cavalry in long lines winding between the magnificent oak and beech trees of which the forest is composed— Abkhasians on wiry ponies dodging in and out, and getting past everybody—mules and pack-horses, in awkward predicaments, stopping up the road, on whose devoted heads were showered an immense variety of oaths by their drivers, who, in their turn, were sworn at by the rest of the world. There were some batteries of artillery, which looked so hopelessly imbedded that nothing short of British energy, as impersonated in Colonel Caddell, who commanded, could have extricated them. There were broken-down baggage-waggons and broken-down mules, and everything but broken-down men. Here and there a pasha was squatted by the roadside indulging in his nargilhe, enjoying his " kief," and watching placidly the exertions of his troops.

At last I got past this scene to a pretty village perched upon the river bank, where the peasants were grouped by the roadside selling

Indian-corn cobs, and cakes made of the same grain or of millet, to the passers-by. Everything was paid for regularly, and the property of the country-people in Abkhasia was scrupulously respected by the Turkish army during its onward progress through the country. Beyond this the road was more open and dry, and the occasional ravines were roughly bridged. I found the *avant poste* encamped in a large plain near the village of Ertiscal, about twenty miles distant from Shemsherrai. It consisted of sixteen battalions of infantry and three battalions of Rifles. On the following morning they received the order to march for the Ingour. Two battalions of Rifles, commanded by Colonel Ballard, led the way, followed by about six thousand infantry and artillery, the whole being under the command of Abdi Pasha. The main body of these troops halted at about an hour's distance from the river, while the Rifles, with two field-pieces and two battalions of infantry, took up a position on a large plain, separated from the river by a belt of wood about half a mile in width.

I esteemed myself fortunate in having received from Colonel Ballard a kind invitation to take up my quarters with him during the campaign, not only because I thus found myself sure of an agreeable companion in a life in which solitude is often most irksome, but because, in attaching myself to the fortunes of the corps he commanded, I was certain not to miss anything worth seeing. The Rifles (about two thousand strong) are the crack troops of the Turkish army, in whose valour, tried in many .hard-fought actions, Omer Pasha deservedly has the utmost confidence; and who, ever placed in the post of danger, have found in the young Englishman who commands them an experienced and gallant leader.

Colonel Simmons paid us a visit in the afternoon, and I accompanied him and Colonel Ballard down to the banks of the Ingour, to have a first glimpse of the Russians. Our guide led us by devious little woodcutters' paths to the river's edge, where, concealed by the thick underwood, we could observe at our leisure the heads of the soldiers above the stockades, and here and there the gleam of a bayonet in the thick wood behind. We had not, however, time for a lengthened inspection, as, the advanced guard being considerably nearer the enemy than to its supports, Colonel Ballard was fully occupied for the rest of the day in securing his position and placing outposts.

The open plain before us, which he carefully divested of clumps of bushes and whatever could offer a shelter, was swept by the guns which had been placed in a little tabia, hastily but skilfully thrown up by the Turkish soldiers, who are adepts at earthworks, and the wood in our rear offered us cover in case of a retreat. The night, however, passed over without an alarm, and on the following morning our little force was doubled.

I was glad to hear from Ballard that I could be of use with my sketch-book in making drawings of the bed of the river and the opposite bank, so I started after breakfast with half-a-dozen riflemen to reconnoitre. As the enemy, upon discovering us, did not seem disposed to offer us any annoyance, I pursued my avocations without taking any particular care to conceal myself. The river was divided by a narrow stony island into two branches, each about thirty yards broad. The opposite bank was densely wooded, and trees had been felled and interlaced with those which were standing, in

F

such a way as to form a most formidable-
looking stockade for more than a mile. 'At
one point there was an earthwork, where thirty
or forty soldiers were collected together ; and
we were staring at one another curiously when
we heard some dropping shots lower down the
river. Shortly afterwards, Ballard appeared with
two companies of Rifles for a little practice, as
the enemy had opened the proceedings. The
only casualty, however, which we had to record,
happened to a poor little boy, about ten years
old, who was a nephew of Prince Michael's,
and who accompanied his younger brother to
the wars. I had remarked the lads, the day
before, dressed in the brilliant and picturesque
costume of Abkhasian beys, armed with minia-
ture - looking daggers and pistols, and surrounded by retainers. The one who was
wounded received a ball in his leg, from the
effects of which I was glad to hear that he
was likely soon to recover.

An intimation, in the shape of a minié
bullet or two, that we were going to favour
my quondam friends on the opposite bank
with more serious attention, soon rendered
them remarkably chary of exposing themselves

—a precaution which, to say the truth, we also adopted. We soon got tired of sneaking about among the bushes, trying to take a dirty advantage of our enemy, and after exchanging a few harmless shots returned to camp, which enabled the Russian general to report officially that his " brisk fire had compelled us to retreat."

My first experience of life in the Turkish camp was most agreeable. The weather for a month past had been cloudless, and the days bright and sunny, but never in the least oppressive — the nights clear and frosty. Our tents were pitched at the edge of the wood, and the thick tendrils of a vine hanging from one tree to another at the door of mine, formed, with the aid of a blanket, a pleasant swing. Having so lately started, we were well supplied with luxuries, and provisions were purchasable in the neighbouring villages. But reconnoitring was more interesting work than foraging, and next day I made another expedition, accompanied by some riflemen, to the river.

This time the enemy were on the alert. Whenever a speck of red was discerned, a shower of bullets informed us of the fact; so we put our Fez caps in our pockets, and crawled about as

if we were deer-stalking. The most exciting
operation was getting from one clump of bushes
to another, when they were separated by the
sandy bed of the river, and completely exposed to observation. We had one or two narrow
escapes, in consequence of the men who were
with me not being able to resist tempting
shots, though I frequently ordered them not to
fire ; the reply from the other side offering a
most unseasonable interruption to my sketch,
and involving a speedy decampment. I must
do one of them the justice to say, that he made
a remarkably good shot, at a distance of about
two hundred yards, as I saw the man he fired
at carried away by his comrades from behind
the corner of the stockade into the wood. Once
my horse, who was concealed in some bushes in
rear, smelt a friend and neighed, when he was
immediately admonished by half-a-dozen balls
whizzing past his nose. In fact, the Russians
kept such an uncommonly good look-out, that
it was sketching under difficulties.

After some trouble, I was fortunate enough to
find the ford. Omer Pasha arrived himself next
morning, and determined to erect two batteries
upon points which commanded it. These were

immediately in face of the Russian stockade ; so it was necessary that the work should be accomplished by night, and with the utmost secresy. As engineer officers are scarce in the Turkish army, or, at all events, as none were forthcoming upon that occasion, Colonel Simmons gave me a lesson in battery-making, and sent me to Skender Pasha to get the men and gabions necessary for one battery, while he superintended the construction of the other. About ten o'clock P.M. I found Skender with his reserves, bivouacked near the wood ; and he, supposing me in the dark to be an officer, gave me, not only a working party of two hundred men, but a regiment of infantry and two field-pieces, a command with which I was considerably astonished and overwhelmed. However, I thought it would scarcely be discreet to undeceive him, so we marched off, and half an hour afterwards were silently and vigorously at work on the bank of the river, within about a hundred yards of the Russian sentries. We had almost filled our front row of gabions when the Turkish major whispered that he saw the Russians coming down to the river in force. This was a most startling announcement. I certainly saw, through the darkness, three black lines drawn up upon the opposite shore. As my experience in military matters was exactly that of most other Lincoln's-Inn barristers, and my knowledge of Turkish did not include a single word of command, the thought of the two field-pieces and the regiment of infantry began rather to trouble me——more particularly as the artillery officer suggested something that I did not in the least understand. However, I peremptorily ordered him not, and discovered, to my intense relief, on looking through my opera-glass, that the Russians were, in fact, three rows of logs, which successive floods had stranded upon the bank.

About one o'clock A.M., when the battery was nearly completed, Simmons and Ballard came to inspect my work ; and finding that my services were no longer needed, I turned campwards, paying a visit *en route* to the other battery, which was about a quarter of a mile lower down the river. This had been a more difficult operation ; not only was the point upon which it was situated nearer to the enemy, but the wood was of a closer and heavier description, involving so much cracking and chopping, in spite of every precaution, that I wondered it had not as yet attracted the Russian fire. Here, as at the other battery, the work was going on busily. I had time now to look on as a spectator at a scene calculated to make a strong impression upon the imagination. The earnest countenances and rapid movements of the men clearly showed that they were working against time. There was still much to be done, and every nerve was strained, every sinew braced, to complete the battery before dawn should disclose it to a lynx-eyed enemy. Here were men clearing the wood and preparing the places for the gabions, others were jamming these side by side, while spades, shovels, and sandbags were in active requisition to fill them with earth. The hurried orders were given, and impatient demands for more gabions made, in whispers. The most profound darkness reigned over all : these men worked like ants, without the glimmer of a torch to light, or even the spark of a pipe to cheer them. Every now and then the challenge of a Russian sentry came across the water to remind us of the necessity of renewed exertion, and the long lines of soldiers bearing gabions seemed never ending as they forced their way along the narrow path.

At last I scrambled past these, and past the sentries, standing watchful and silent at short intervals, until I once again reached the reserve, and was not sorry to seat myself on a drum by the side of Skender Pasha and a crackling fire. He was much amused when I enlightened him as to my real calling in life, and we had a pleasant chat about the excitements and vicissitudes of a soldier's career, of which there is probably no man living whose experience has a wider range. I am afraid to say where this gallant old Pole has not fought ; but he assured me that he had eighteen serious wounds, not counting the loss of some fingers, and others of a light and trivial nature. There certainly was a hole in his head which looked as if nobody who was not accustomed to being seriously wounded could have received it and lived. Skender keeps that part of his head shaved, and has an excusable trick of pushing his fez back in an inadvertent manner. It was nearly morning before I got back to my tent, with its comfortable bed of fern, in which my Circassian servant used nightly to litter me down; and I was just dropping off to sleep, when a series of sharp reports informed me that one of the batteries had been discovered; so I dozed uneasily till daylight, when, the firing still continuing, I went down to see what was going on. I just reached Simmons' battery as a poor fellow was knocked over, shot through the heart. For the most part, however, the shot struck harmlessly upon the outside of the gabions, and the men were seated under them, smoking or chatting, and in comparative security. There was only one unfinished corner where exposure was still necessary. However, the battery was completed without further loss, and I then paid a visit to mine, and found it in a very advanced and satisfactory state. The guns were not put into either until the following night. During the day nothing was done—it was one of the most perfect repose; so I devoted myself to my vine swing, with a presentiment that it was only the lull which precedes the storm.

The whole army had now come up. Upon

a hill commanding the river, about half a mile
to our left, one battalion of Rifles, some infantry
and artillery, were placed.   On our right came
the division of Skender Pasha, while about a
mile to the right rear of him, Omer Pasha, with
the main body of the army, was encamped. It
consisted altogether of four brigades (thirty-
two battalions) of infantry, four battalions of
Rifles, and one thousand cavalry, with twenty-
seven field-pieces and ten mountain-guns, or in
all about twenty thousand men. The remainder
of the force, about ten thousand men, were
employed protecting the depôts which had been
established at Godova, Shemsherrai, and Souchoum.

There were a suspicious number of messages
flying about all day.   Aides-du-camp pulled
up their panting horses at Ballard's tent, and
his bimbashis seemed to me greater bores than
usual.   The habit of a Turkish subordinate
officer is to pay his superior interminable visits.
He sits on his heels, smokes the colonel's tobacco,
and talks platitudes and bravado by the hour,
believing that he is thereby obtaining his favour.
He always fawns, generally begs, and is perfectly

incapable of taking a hint that his presence has become a nuisance. I must make an exception in favour of one Rifle bimbashi, whose only request was, that if we fought on the following day, his battalion should lead the way. Thus the day of a commanding officer in the Turkish army is in great part spent in receiving the visits of his subordinates. Just before dark the roll is called, when the men go to dinner. It is the most impressive moment of the day in a Turkish camp. Regiment after regiment blesses the Sultan with three cheers of gratitude. We used first to hear the distant shouts of Skender's division, as, sitting in the cool evening, they were borne to us on the gentle breeze. Scarcely audible at first, each regiment along the line took up the melodious cheer, until the stentorian lungs of our own corps rent the air; then it died away on the extreme left, and the men became absorbed in beans and biscuit. After this the shades of evening close in upon us, and fires are made before the tents of the commanding officers, who sit near them, and hold a levee over coffee and pipes. We were engaged in this laudable occupation about six

P.M., when the order came to extinguish all camp-fires and lights. This looked serious, so, as we could not see to read, and got very cold, we speculated on its import for a short time, and then turned in, full of hope for stirring events on the morrow.

CHAPTER VII.

BEFORE dawn upon the morning of the 6th of November the Rifles were under arms. We had received orders to be at the camp of the Sirdar Ekrem (commander-in-chief) at daylight, and we found his Highness seated by the fire before his tent waiting for us. The plain behind was a scene of universal stir and bustle. Troops were collecting in different directions, and getting into the order of march; and in less than an hour the whole army (with the exception of Skender Pasha's division), consisting of about fifteen thousand men, was advancing in a westerly direction, and parallel with the Ingour. It was evident that we were destined to turn the Russian position at Roukhi, and cross the river by a ford lower down.

It was a lovely morning; and as I accompanied the army on its march across the charming country—now through noble forests, now over plains dotted with magnificent timber, past picturesque villages and Indian-corn fields, where the peasants collected to see us, and listened wonderingly to the stirring strains of each regiment as it marched past—I thought I had never enjoyed a morning ride more thoroughly, for with the charms of this novel and inspiriting scene was combined the impatient excitement of anticipation.

At last, after advancing for about seven miles, the troops debouched upon a plain near the river, and Omer Pasha and his staff drew up to inspect them for the last time before they crossed. Then he sent forward Colonel Ballard in command of the advanced guard, composed of three battalions and a half of Rifles and four guns, to lead the way across a branch of the river to a long narrow island, near the other extremity of which we hoped to find a ford. Our information, however, was somewhat vague, as it had been derived from peasants, upon whom implicit confidence was scarcely to be placed, and who were now serving as guides. We found the island covered with a thick copse-wood, through which we pursued a narrow path,

Ballard throwing out skirmishers on both sides. The main body of the army followed at no great distance in rear.

After having proceeded through the wood for about two miles, we entered a plain at mid-day, and were immediately and un-expectedly greeted by a pretty sharp fire of musketry and a few round shot. The latter, we observed, proceeded from a battery about six hundred yards distant, upon the opposite side of the river ; the former from a wood immediately facing us, at the other end of the plain, about a hundred yards distant. As the Rifles crossed this open ground with great rapidity, the fire ceased, and Ballard found himself in possession of the wood without diffi-culty. Notwithstanding the tremendous fire of grape and musketry which was opened upon him from the battery upon the other side, he at once proceeded, followed by Mr Longworth, whose warlike propensities had been thoroughly developed in the Hungarian war of '48, to search for a ford. In this he was unsuccessful. He therefore applied himself to returning the fire of the battery with interest.

Meanwhile Colonel Simmons, who had hitherto

accompanied the Rifles, thought it advisable to discover a path, by which the rest of the army could reach the wood without being exposed to the fire of the fort. I went to assist in the search, and we found comparative shelter in the bed of the branch we had already crossed. At this point the island was not more than fifty yards across. We then joined Omer, who was coming up with the artillery, which he drew up on the plain, and which, under the able direction of Colonel Caddell, who was the second in command, opened a well-aimed fire upon the battery. This had been a good deal interrupted by the fire of the Rifles, whose minié bullets were insinuating themselves into the embrasures with immense effect.

Still the Russian guns managed to do us some damage. Colonel Caddell had dismounted, and was holding his horse, and talking to a Pasha, when a round shot came between them, went through his horse, killed his interpreter, and hopped into the ranks of a regiment in rear, doing a good deal of mischief, and finally disappeared down the bank, followed by the Pasha, whom I did not again observe on the field. Omer remained for some time near this

ear

in

Steep bank with abattis

Dry bed of stream

Forest with

openings

Some of Osman's
Division after cross
marching to thei

Slippery stony bottom

Route of Osman Pasha's column which crossed 1¾ miles
lower down opposed by 2 batts of Russians.

battery, and directed some of the guns himself.
Then we rode about the field for no particular
object—apparent to a civilian, at any rate.
Mr Longworth, who had returned from the
front, saw that there was a great deal more
doing there, so we rode back to see how Ballard
was getting on.   He had lost upwards of a
hundred men in killed and wounded, which
was not to be wondered at, considering the
peppering they had been exposed to for
about three hours.   However, they had the
satisfaction of knowing that they were doing
good service ; their fire turned out afterwards to have proved most deadly.

Too much credit cannot be given to Ballard
for the manner in which he got his men into
position.   They lined the very water's edge,
taking advantage of every bush and stump
to conceal themselves ; and, lying behind
fallen logs, they concentrated their fire upon
embrasures as the guns were being loaded,
picked off the artillery - horses by dozens,
which the Russians kept unaccountably inside
the battery, and did immense execution generally.   Whenever Ballard saw a man unwill-
ing to take up his position near the edge of

G

the river, he pricked him, not with his sword's point, but with that sharper weapon which a Turk fears more — quiet irony. "Make a gabion of me, my good fellow ; put your gun on my shoulder, and then you're sure not to be hit," was a home-thrust which irresistibly impelled the object of it forward. There were two or three cottages in the wood which were turned into a temporary hospital, and here I saw numbers of poor fellows patiently suffering, or as resignedly expiring. Mules with litters stood under the sheltered side, and one by one disappeared, each with his melancholy load.

Meantime the Rifles were running short of ammunition, and the 4th regiment was sent down to their support. These men, headed by a gallant old Turk near seventy years of age, whose bravery as an officer would have distinguished him anywhere, but made him a positive curiosity in the Turkish army, dashed into the wood with cheers of Allah ! to Ballard's astonishment, passed over the almost prostrate forms of his skilful riflemen, and drew up in line on the river-bank outside the wood. It was not until they had fired a volley into the battery, and were beginning to feel the effect of their unprotected position, that Ballard could induce the old colonel to retire into the wood, and make him understand that it was his duty, under the circumstances, to conceal, and not expose his men.

The roll of small-arms and the booming of artillery had been going on fitfully for some hours ; it was drawing towards evening, and as yet there was no apparent result. I began to think that we might fail after all ; but seeing a number of troops marching past in rear of the wood, Mr Longworth suggested that they might be going to try some other ford ; so we left the Rifles and followed Osman Pasha, who commanded the division. After marching for about a mile and a half down the island, we crossed a small branch to another island, then to a third, and found that we were separated from the opposite shore by a narrow, but deep and swift stream. As the troops dashed across this, they were received, as they reached the shore, by a sharp fire, which killed and wounded about a hundred and fifty men ; but as they still pressed on, the Russians did not stay to receive the shock, but dispersed precipitately into the woods.

Osman Pasha's brigade was about five thousand strong ; the force opposed to us, we supposed, consisted of about fifteen hundred men ; but it was reported, I know not with what truth, that two new battalions and three field-pieces had arrived at this point before we crossed— we certainly heard nothing of the latter. We were just beginning to take up a position upon our newly-won territory, when, to my astonishment, a series of cheers were faintly borne to us upon the still air of evening, for it was now nearly dark. This was the announcement that the battery had been taken ; but how the operation had been managed was a mystery to us, as, when we left, it seemed madness to have attempted the ford, which the earthwork had been erected to command.

It was some satisfaction, after the sustained excitement consequent upon the day's proceedings, to stretch one's self near a blazing wood-fire, and rest one's weary limbs, and talk over our successes. The party consisted of Osman Pasha, a genuine Turk, and abominator of

Giaours ; Ferhad Pasha, whose Frank name of Stein speaks for itself, and who has served in almost every army in the world ; Issac Bey, a handsome young Circassian chief, who had been *en amateur* wherever the fire was hottest during the fight, and whose project of a visit to England, at the Duke of Newcastle's invitation, came to an untimely end, for he died, on the retreat, of typhus fever, brought on by hardship and exposure. Mr Longworth and myself completed the circle. We shared a very small allowance of rice, which Osman Pasha generously distributed, and which was most acceptable, as I had tasted nothing since the night before. Then we lighted our pipes, and under the genial influence of *sou à la Franca (Anglicè* brandy-and-water), and a consciousness of having distinguished himself, Osman condescended to be gracious, and entertained us with his deeds of valour ; but by far the most amusing companion amongst the Turkish generals was Ferhad Pasha, whose society whiled away many a tedious hour.

We pulled down a stack of Indian-corn stalks, and strewed them for a bed. During this time the men had been collecting the wounded ;

and as ours was the most comfortable blaze,
many of the poor creatures were laid near it
to die.   I never saw anything more patient
than both Russians and Turks under suffering.
Here they were lying side by side without
uttering a complaint, except now and then,
when, in turning, one would move the wounded
limb of another.   Then there would come the
look of agony and the sharp cry of pain; but
the old expression would return again in a
moment——in the Russian, one of dogged sul-
lenness; in the Turk, of patient resignation.
When they died, they were carried away, and
others brought to fill their places; and so,
during all that long bitterly cold night, these
suffering beings were lying on the opposite
side of the fire; but though often roused for an
instant from my restless sleep, in which the
bloodless countenances of these men haunted
my imagination, I never heard a groan to
give the force of reality to my dreams.

Although the fire was kept in all night, and
I was lying jammed tightly in between Ferhad
Pasha and Mr Longworth, the two biggest men
of the party, not having even a greatcoat to cover
me, I was very cold and stiff next morning;

and, indeed, the thick hoar-frost on the ground left no other result to be expected. At daylight the artillery and cavalry came across the river. The exertions of Abdullah Pasha, who commanded the former, were worthy of all praise. In getting his guns up the steep and muddy bank, the horses constantly fell, and we had to put on a large force of men to pull them out of the mess. At last we were all ready, as we supposed, for a start : the troops were fresh ; they had done but little fighting ; the cavalry had not drawn a sabre ; and we expected momentarily to receive an order from Omer Pasha to go in pursuit. This, however, not arriving, Mr Longworth and I determined to ride up to the battery upon the same side of the river.

For about a mile our way led us upon the track of the flying Russians. The scent was evidently hot—knapsacks, greatcoats, broken muskets, &c., were strewn about, and afforded interesting subjects for the inspection of Mr L.'s Albanian servant, who was addicted to lagging a little behind on such occasions. At last we began to doubt whether we had not missed our way to the battery, and as we were quite alone, we contemplated the possibility of our

falling ingloriously into the hands of the
retreating Muscovites with disquietude. We
were just preparing to turn back when a horse-
man appeared, who turned out to be an aide-
de-camp from Omer Pasha, who put the same
question to us which we did to him, and with
no doubt the same anxiety depicted in his
countenance. However, we mutually relieved
each other's doubts, and a few minutes afterwards the signs and evidences of another battle-
field met our gaze.

As we emerged from the forest upon an
open plain, we saw before us the battery which
had given us so much trouble upon the previous day, filled with the carcasses of men and
horses. Among the latter especially great execution seemed to have been done. Upwards
of sixty lay heaped together within the small
area of the battery, while the bodies of Russian soldiers who had fallen were being hastily
stripped and buried. The majority of these, however, were found in the wood, and the report of
the number buried before evening amounted to
about four hundred. Among these, two were
colonels, and six inferior officers. There, too,
stood three guns and seven ammunition-wag-

gons, the trophies of the fight. In one of the latter I counted twenty-seven minié bullet-marks, which gave indisputable evidence of the hot fire to which their defenders had been exposed, and of the gallantry with which they had so long maintained the position.

Omer Pasha had not yet crossed the river, so Mr Longworth went to discover his headquarters, whilst I proceeded to institute anxious inquiries after Ballard, whose instinct I knew always led him into the hottest fire ; while the peculiar satisfaction he seemed to feel at finding himself there always induced him to remain : I therefore almost despaired of seeing him again alive. While prowling about looking at the melancholy relics of the battle, and almost expecting to find him among them, I observed an English officer, whom I did not know, as he had only made his appearance the day before (and who left the army the day after), seated under a hedge deep in the mysteries of a *paté de fois gras*. After an almost uninterrupted fast of thirty-six hours I required no other introduction, and, jumping off my horse, seized upon half of it, to which I am bound to say I was made cordially welcome. My pleasure at hearing that Ballard was safe was damped by the melancholy intelligence that Captain Dymock, Colonel Simmons' aide-de-camp, had fallen near the spot where we then were, and had since died of his wound. I immediately rode to headquarters to hear more fully the particulars of this part of the day's proceedings.

Omer Pasha had taken possession of a cottage in the wood, and was busily engaged in writing his despatches. It appeared that at about 4 P.M. Colonel Simmons had suggested the propriety of his endeavouring to ford the river higher up, so as to take the battery in reverse. Of this suggestion Omer Pasha approved, and, accompanied by Captain Dymock and his interpreter, Hidaiot, he succeeded in leading two battalions of infantry and three companies of Rifles across to the opposite bank. The current was so swift, however, that in effecting this operation about half-a-dozen men were swept from their legs, carried down the stream, and drowned. Upon entering the wood, the small party found a cart-track, along which they proceeded to a ditch, upon the opposite side of

which an abattis of bushes had been placed.
Not suspecting an attack from this quarter,
this was not defended, and, leaving a reserve
here, Colonel Simmons passed through it without the enemy being aware of his presence.
When, however, he was within about six hundred yards of the battery, he was perceived,
and charged by a Russian column, who were
met by a heavy fire. At this moment a
second column attacked them in flank, and
Colonel Simmons, collecting a few men, turned
to meet them, leaving Dymock and Hidaiot to
charge through the first column into the battery. In the brief but hot struggle which en-
sued, in which the Turks lost about fifty men
in killed and wounded, Captain Dymock's
horse was shot under him whilst he was gal-
lantly cheering them on; and at almost the
same moment a ball struck him in the chest,
and wounded him mortally. Hidaiot quickly
took his place : with his red cap trimmed with
fur, his Polish military cloak, he was scarcely
recognisable from a Russian officer. Being a
Pole, he had served for many years in the
armies of the Czar. His knowledge of Russian
now stood him in good stead. Making his voice

heard above the din of battle, " my children," he called out to the Russian soldiers who were hemming in the small band on all sides, " fly; my children, you are surrounded—whole regiments of these infidels are coming through the wood." In another moment he found the battery deserted; and touching the guns with his sword as a sign that he was their captor, this brave fellow returned to attend upon poor Dymock, who breathed his last in his arms. For his gallant conduct upon this occasion Hidaiot was made a major in the army, and received the order of the Mejidie.

In the afternoon, thirty or forty Russian prisoners were brought up for examination. They were miserable, half-starved-looking men. I wondered the more at the determination of the defence when I saw those by whom it had been made. Some of these were Tartars from Kazan, and consequently Mahommedans; but they were all soldiers of the line. They reported that the force which had been opposed to us consisted of eight battalions of infantry (about five thousand men), three thousand Georgian militia, eight guns, and seven thousand volunteers. The volunteers, however, vanished into the woods as soon as the first round-shot whistled over their heads. The prisoners were well treated, and seemed perfectly contented with their lot. The wounded shared the attentions of the English surgeons with the Turks. Only two of these gentlemen, Dr. Edwards and Mr Turner, were with the army, and during a great part of the day they were engaged in their laborious duties under the fire of the enemy. Upon them alone, in fact, devolved the entire charge of the wounded. We afterwards heard from reliable authority that the loss of the Russians in this battle amounted to about twelve hundred in killed and wounded; that of the Turks did not reach four hundred. It is impossible to speak too highly of the gallantry which the Turkish soldiers displayed throughout the action. Not only did the Rifles exhibit the utmost steadiness while exposed for upwards of six hours to the fire of the battery, but those infantry who took the battery by assault dashed forward with all the bravery and *élan* of the Zouaves. It is in this latter quality that the Turks have been supposed deficient; but they showed, both under Osman Pasha and Colonel Simmons, that they possess it in a far higher degree that the Russians, and indeed as fully as any troops in the world.

A characteristic anecdote is told of one of the soldiers who was the first to set foot inside the battery. Perceiving a Russian colonel lying dead upon the ground, he plucked off his glove and appropriated a valuable diamond ring which was upon his finger. Knowing, however, that it would be impossible very long to keep secret the possession of so valuable a prize, he showed his usbashi, or captain, his treasure, and requested permission to keep it. The usbashi told the man that he was quite right to bring the prize to him, and that henceforward it should be transferred to the finger of the said usbashi. The soldier, not satisfied with this arrangement, referred the matter to the bimbashi, or major, who said that both he and the usbashi were highly culpable in daring to retain the ring from their superior officer, and that he would therefore relieve them of the subject of dispute. From the bimbashi the soldier went to the kaima-kama, or lieutenant-colonel, who at once followed the example of his inferiors, and took possession of the ring. The soldier still persevered, however, and went to the meer-ali (colonel), who determined that he was the rightful possessor of the ring by virtue of his rank, and dismissed the rival claimants from his presence in the most summary manner. Next day a French officer attached to the staff of Omer Pasha observed a private soldier prowling near the tent of the commander-in-chief. The story of the ring was at once retailed by its original possessor to this gentleman, who laid the matter before his Highness, and the man had not only the satisfaction of regaining possession of his property, but of knowing that those who had attempted successively to deprive him of it had been severely reprimanded for their conduct.

Of the Turkish officers generally, the less said the better. Nobody takes much notice of them while fighting is going on ; and indeed it is only then, when, in the excitement of the moment, men from Omer Pasha downwards speak the languages which are most familiar to them all, that one discovers how many foreigners there are in the Turkish army, and how really dependent that army is for its triumphs upon them. Before the day closed we had the melancholy duty to perform of burying poor Dymock. His grave was dug within a few yards of the spot where he fell, between two noble trees, and over the little green mound, the graceful branches of a wild vine clinging to them both, formed a natural arch.

Captain Dymock's Grave.

CHAPTER VIII.

HAVING upon the second night after the battle dined and slept at head-quarters, when Omer Pasha received a flying visit from Mr Danby Seymour, I joined Ballard on the following morning as he was going to accompany Colonel Simmons upon a reconnaissance, which was pushed as far as Sugdidi, a distance of twelve miles. We left our camp upon the Ingour with two battalions of Rifles and two regiments of cavalry. The country in the immediate neighbourhood of the river is thickly wooded, but the winding paths by which it is threaded soon join the main road from the coast to Sugdidi, which is as broad and smooth as a bowling-green, and which traverses extensive plains of clover, wild carrots, thyme, and fern. We left the Rifles in a wood at the edge of one of these, and proceeded along this road with the cavalry only.   Quantities of dead horses, some scarcely cold, showed how recent had been the Russian retreat.   A shot soon after warned us that we were in an enemy's country; and we found, upon galloping up to the advanced guard, that they had come upon four Mingrelian militia, of whom one was lying dead at our feet.   As we approached the town, we were repeatedly fired upon from the woods, but without effect; and as we rode into it, we saw a small party of fifteen or twenty mounted Cossacks, who immediately took to their heels.   We found the town completely deserted; but five or six Mingrelian soldiers were made prisoners in the neighbourhood.   They informed us that the nearest Russian force was at a village about three hours' distance, where there was also a large depôt of provisions.

We had no time then to continue our explorations; so having made prize of a goose and a quantity of potatoes, we turned homewards. We found the Rifles waiting for us.   They had been laid out to the right and left of the road in skirmishing order, and made good use of the opportunity which was thus afforded of appropriating the poultry that inhabited the otherwise deserted cottages; and as we marched back, a constant cackling proceeded from the ranks, and the inquisitive-looking beaks of cocks and hens protruded themselves from coat-pockets, in spite of the anxiety of the owner of the prize to keep its possession a secret.

We lost our way in the woods when darkness came on, and after their hard day's fighting the day before, the men stumbled along the muddy road a good deal fatigued. We ultimately struck the camp, where we were not expected; and as a specimen of Turkish vigilance, we marched into it at nine o'clock P.M., about two thousand strong, without ever having received a challenge. Our tents had not come across the river, so we bivouacked near the battery, and discussed our proceedings over our camp-fire. It was some consolation, however, to find ourselves at last fairly in Mingrelia. We could scarcely be said before to have entered the country, as the province of Samoursachan, which we had just left, had been a continual subject of dispute between the Dadians of Mingrelia and the Princes of Abkhasia. At last, Russia was called in to mediate, and satisfactorily settled

H

the matter by appropriating the entire revenue
of the province, thereby rendering its proprie-
torship valueless.   The rival claimants were
not, after the oyster was swallowed, awarded
even a shell each.

We had now been forty-eight hours upon
the field of battle, and the Russians had consequently gained a clear start of two days.   This
was very provoking ; but civilians generally
grumble at military arrangements, about which
they are supposed to know nothing ; so I con-
clude there was some good reason for it, which
I have never yet discovered.   Had we not
again waited five days at Sugdidi, I should
have supposed that the commissariat arrangements necessitated this delay.   But that can
scarcely have been the case, as Sugdidi was
only four miles, by the direct road, farther
from our base of operations.

Just as we were going to sleep, an order came
from the commander-in-chief that the Rifles
were not to make such a noise.   They had
begun to quarrel over their fowls, and, as is
usual among the bravest troops, they were by
far the most disorderly set in the Turkish
army.   However, Omer petted them no more

than they deserved ; and if they had not pos-
sessed inexhaustible spirits, they never could
have undergone the work they did. Ballard
was immensely popular among them. They
highly appreciated his perfect coolness and
self-possession under fire ; and the night of
the battle he made them a speech, in which
he informed them, in a few flattering sentences,
that they, with the assistance of a few regiments of infantry, had won the day ; which
was true enough ; but for a colonel to make a
speech to his men was altogether an innova-
tion in the Turkish army, and one which, to
judge from its effect, might be introduced with
advantage.

Upon the following morning, the whole army
moved to Sugdidi. The greatest terror of the
Turks seemed to prevail among the inhabitants,
and the country was entirely depopulated. The
consequence was, that, in spite of Omer Pasha's
earnest endeavours to reassure the people, and
to prevent pillage, a desultory plundering went
on. It is only fair, however, to the Turkish
soldiery to say that the irregular Abkhasian
cavalry, of whom about two hundred were
attached to the army, were the principal ag-

gressors.   They seem, as far as my observation
of them went, to have all the vices, without
any of the virtues, of bashi-bazouks.

Sugdidi is the principal town of Mingrelia.
It is situated upon a gentle eminence, which
overlooks a rich country, and to the right of
which extends a vast level plain, where the army
is now encamped. The town itself is composed
of two streets of wooden houses, shaded by
avenues of beech trees.   A week before, it probably contained about two thousand inhabitants ; when we arrived, there was not a living
creature to be seen in it, except a few stray
curs, who must, before our arrival, have been
excessively astonished at finding themselves
the only inhabitants of a once bustling town.
The streets run into a square, upon one side of
which is situated the magnificent residence of
the Princess Dadian, only one wing of which
is completed, while the other two are composed
of the Greek church and its adjacent buildings,
and the picturesque wooden residence of Prince
Gregoire.

We entered the palace of the Princess, and
found the most magnificent collection of furni-
ture in the drawing-room.   It was clear, from

the number of articles of value which had
been left behind, that her Highness had calculated upon a more protracted resistance on the
part of the Russians than had been made.   A
very handsome picture of the Emperor Nicholas
was still in its case, and had evidently been
packed, but considered not worth carrying
away under the circumstances.   Chairs and
couches covered with crimson velvet, beautiful
inlaid tables, magnificent chandeliers, and articles of vertu, which looked like late importa-
tions from Paris, were all so carefully arranged
that he would have been a ruthless conqueror
who could have destroyed them.   After satis-
fying his curiosity, Omer Pasha accordingly
placed guards at all the entrances to the palace,
and to the gardens, which were extremely beautiful, and laid out with great taste.   There were
the choicest flowers in great profusion, and extensive fruit-gardens and orangeries, while the
deer and pea-fowl wandered about completely
their own masters.   Having once penetrated
into the mysteries of this fairyland, it was somewhat annoying to find that, though my tent
was pitched at the gate, I was debarred, like
my neighbours, from re-entering it by an in-

flexible sentry, otherwise I should assuredly
have adopted the summer-house in the flower-
garden, which I used to look at with longing
eyes, as a smoking-room.

The Princess Dadian, who is said to have
been very beautiful, was married to Prince
Dadian, who had by her one son.   Since
the death of her husband she has been
acting as regent for this boy, who is about
eight years old.   Her husband had two bro-
thers, Constantine and Gregoire, both of whom
fled with their sister-in-law to her residence
in the mountains.   Upon the arrival of Omer
Pasha, a few peasants who had been taken
prisoners were sent home, and told that their
property and countrymen would be respected
everywhere by the Turkish army.   Sentries
were posted at the church and in the streets,
to prevent any one even from entering them ;
and so strict were the orders against plunder of any sort that no shooting was allowed near the camp, which, considering
the quantities of woodcocks and pheasants
in the woods, and the great scarcity of
animal diet, was rather a privation.   I used,
however, to break through this rule occa-

sionally. As the people regained confidence, we visited their villages, and got them to show us good ground for woodcock and pheasants at some distance from the town. When they found we were harmless sportsmen, they were generally civil, and sold us poultry. In some villages the inhabitants were foolish enough not to come back ; and then, of course, if they would leave poultry behind them, and were not there to take the money, we could not help it.

The Abkhasians, however, used to perpetrate thefts of a much more serious nature, and perhaps one could scarcely blame the country people for keeping out of the way. These lawless foragers indulged chiefly in the plunder of human beings. Arriving in a village, their appearance would strike terror into the breasts of the women and infuriate the men. Seizing the handsomest boys and the prettiest girls, they would tear them shrieking from their agonised parents, and, swinging them on their saddle-bow, gallop away with them through the forest, followed by the cries and execrations of the whole population. It was said, I know not with what truth, that sixty persons had been kidnapped near Sugdidi during our stay there. Indeed, so monstrous did the evil become, that Omer, after bastinadoing three of the offenders before his tent, despatched the whole of the Abkhasian contingent, to the number of about two hundred, back to their own country.

Meantime, Prince Michael, who had been allowed perfect liberty, but at the same time kept under a respectable sort of surveillance, asked permission to go to visit his sister-in-law the Princess, ostensibly with a view of persuading her to follow his example, and espouse the cause of the Turks. There can be no doubt that had she done so, and placed the resources of the country at our disposal, we should not have been subjected to those detentions which were the immediate cause of the failure of the whole campaign. Mr Longworth offered to write to the Princess, who was ignorant of the presence of an English commissioner with the army ; and it is much to be regretted that his Highness did not avail himself of this offer. From Sugdidi all the commissariat animals had to be sent back to Godava, a distance of forty miles, for provisions. The delay of five days here could not, therefore, have been avoided.

There were only fifteen hundred transport-horses for the whole army. This was certainly an inadequate supply. At the same time, the weather was then so beautiful that we might have continued our march without tents, and thereby rendered available the services of a thousand more baggage-animals; or if the whole army was unable to go in pursuit of the Russians, a division might have pushed on without very much risk, considering the utterly demoralised state of the enemy's troops. That every day was of the utmost value, was subsequently proved by the fact, that if we had arrived upon the banks of the Skeniscal two days earlier, we should have reached Kutais in twenty-four hours afterwards.

I rode down to the old fortress of Roukhi one day to look at the ford by which Skender Pasha crossed the river, and to command which we had erected the two batteries two days before the battle of the Ingour. It was matter of congratulation that Omer Pasha did not attempt the passage here with his whole army. Although the ford was not commanded by any Russian artillery, the thick woods had been made available in every direction for riflemen, and an abattis had been thrown up at every angle of the narrow road which winds up a steep hill past the old castle. For more than a mile there was scarcely a point which was not swept from some stockade concealed in the woods, and which we only discovered in the course of our explorations. The castle itself is a picturesque old ruin, of great extent, and its ivy-grown towers, surrounded by massive loopholed walls, rise high above the surrounding forest, and form a charming feature in the landscape. It is said to have served formerly as the treasury of the Dadian princes. When the Turks became masters of the country, they placed a garrison in it, but it was dismantled by the Russians in 1770.

Skender Pasha had only two men wounded at this point, while the river was being crossed by us lower down. Two days afterwards he passed over to find the opposite shore deserted.

CHAPTER IX.

HAD we not been most anxious to follow the retreating Russians, Sugdidi was such a delightful spot that we should have looked forward to leaving it with regret. The whole army was encamped in beautiful order upon the vast plain stretching away from the town in a south-westerly direction. The view from the front line was striking. In the foreground, the white tents of the Mussulman host extended far and wide; behind them rose the green dome of the Christian Church, and the avenue of trees marked the streets of the deserted town; while above all towered the snowy peaks of the Caucausian chain, rising to a height of seventeen thousand feet. Skender Pasha had been sent on in command of the advanced guard, and on the 15th the camp was struck, and the whole army was on the march, the Rifles, as usual, leading the way.

We marched through an undulating well-wooded country, along a very fair road, to command which, we observed that stockades had been constructed in available positions. Had the Russians adopted this style of harassing warfare instead of risking a general action on the Ingour, there can be no doubt that they might have inflicted great loss upon us during our march through the country. Leaving the main body of the army to camp some miles in rear, we pushed on to Chetha, where extensive barracks and depôts of provisions had been constructed by the Russians. It is quite possible that, had we pushed on here rapidly after the Ingour, we might have saved these from destruction. As it was, however, the Russians had time to burn them, and we pitched our camp upon about two acres of ground covered with the still smouldering embers of these buildings.

The growing confidence of the population was testified by the fact, that the inhabitants of some of the houses by the roadside had not quitted them upon the approach of the army, although they could not be induced to minister to our wants, protesting that the Russians, before leaving, had appropriated all their live stock. Omer Pasha had given strict orders that no force was to be used in procuring supplies of this nature ; but I found, in the course of my own foraging expeditions, that in many instances the fowls said to be in Muscovite hands were snugly stowed away in some obscure outhouse, and upon the production of some bright silver sixpences, and the assurance that I was an Englishman, a Christian, and no Turk, were readily parted with. In the neighbourhood of our camp was a picturesque old ruin, said to have been the monastery which was formerly tenanted by the Capuchin friars of Mingrelia. It was built in an oval form, about one hundred and fifty yards long by one hundred wide, with three towers, two of which were in a very tolerable state of preservation, and a crumbling ivy-covered archway.

On the following day we marched for three hours to the Chopi. The country became more beautiful as we advanced, and a lovely view burst upon us as we reached the river and

saw the monastery of Chopi perched upon a
bank about three hundred feet high, overhanging the stream. We ascended the steep
hill, and, pitching our tents upon its summit,
revelled in a glorious prospect. To the left,
a richly-wooded plain extended, without an
undulation, to the Black Sea, too distant to
be visible. On the right we saw the broad
fertile valley of the Chopi winding away to
the base of the Caucasian range, where fields
of yellow stubble bore testimony to its abundant cultivation. Villages clustered among
the woods which clothed the hill-sides. These
sometimes swelled gently back, at others terminated abruptly with a precipitous bank,
which was reflected in the blue water at its
base, until they gradually assumed a bolder
character, and became at last lofty mountains, to be in their turn overtopped by the
snow-clad peak of Elbruz. Immediately below us all is bustle and activity. The artillery
is fording the river, and the opposite plain is
alive with troops, pitching their tents or collecting round their camp-fires.

Having feasted our eyes with the view, we
go to inspect the monastery, and find it en-

closed by a crumbling wall, oval in shape, like the one before mentioned ; but the tower here is surmounted by an octagonal belfry.

The Monastery is inhabited by some monks of the Georgian Greek Church of the order of St Basil. One venerable old man, who was the archimandrite, showed Omer Pasha over the establishment. The walls were composed of a most singular collection of fragments of other edifices. Byzantine columns, Corinthian capitals, marble blocks ornamented with paintings by Georgian artists, and remains of frescoes, which originally decorated some other edifice, were all built in together, and combine to invest the whole building with a remarkably faded and patched look. It was evidently very old, but our venerable cicerone presumed somewhat too largely on our credulity when he assured us that it was built eight thousand years ago ! Dubois de Montpereux is probably nearer the mark when he ascribes it to the thirteenth century. It was, according to him, one of the six bishoprics which, of the twelve which Mingrelia formerly contained, were changed into abbeys.

The incongruous materials of which the

church is built were brought from Circassia by Dadian Wamek, about the end of the twelfth century, when he returned from chastising the Circassians. There is an inscription in Mosaic over the doorway to that effect. After describing the successes he achieved and the difficulties which he overcame, the inscription concludes by saying, that this pious Prince "raised these columns and these pieces of marble, and placed here the coffin and the bones of his father and of his mother. It is good to think of them a moment."

In the night we were alarmed by the firing of cannon, as far as we could make out, in the direction of Skender Pasha's brigade, which was two hours in advance ; but, as this turned out not to be the case, on the following morning, it was attributed to Mustapha Pasha, whose troops were supposed not very far distant, in a south-westerly direction.

On the 17th we made a short march, and soon after leaving Chopi, struck the macadamised road which connects Redoute Kaleh with Kutais and Tiflis. Our route from Sugdidi took a direction considerably to the south of that which would have led us straight to Kutais. The advantage, however, of keeping as near the coast as possible was evident, as we were at once enabled to open our communication direct with Redoute Kaleh. By these means supplies reached the army in one day from the sea. We encamped at Choloni upon a hill which overlooked the plain of the Rhion, beyond which rose the snowy mountains of Uzurghetti; behind us the white peaks of the Caucasus were sharply defined against the clear sky. Our weather had hitherto been so unusually lovely that the country people believed that we had Providence in our favour. We saw numerous marks of a recent Russian camp in the neighbourhood, and heard that they were only three hours distant; but they kept pace in their movements with our marches, and retired regularly as we advanced.

On the 18th we continued our march along a magnificent road; the bridges, however, were almost universally destroyed; and, notwithstanding the activity of the Turkish artillery-horses, and the excellent way in which they were managed, there was occasionally some diffi-

I

culty in getting the guns across the ravines and muddy streams with which the road was intersected.

The enchanting weather, added to the beauty of the scenery through which we passed, rendered campaigning in Mingrelia a most agreeable occupation. Our road skirted the base of the spurs which project from the Caucasian chain far into the plains, watered by the Rhion and its tributaries. The wooded hills on our left were generally more or less conical in form, and their summits were almost invariably crowned by the wooden walls of some old monastery, or the massive battlements of a ruined fortress. On the right, richly wooded plains stretched away to the sea ; and church towers rose above the trees, to remind us that the vast and apparently silent forest was indeed inhabited by a Christian population.

We found our camping-ground at the Russian post of Sakharbet, upon the river Ziewie. It was a charming spot. After its rapid and boisterous course from the range in which it rises, the river here takes its last leap over a ledge of rocks twelve or fourteen feet in height, and henceforth winding peacefully through fertile plains, it falls at last into the Rhion. Upon a hill above the river is a ruined castle, and immediately below the waterfall is a little island, upon which stands a piece of crumbling but massive masonry, the remains of some ancient bridge, which has withstood the shock of many a boiling flood. There was very little water in the river now, and it scarcely reached to the knees of the men as they waded through it.

We found Skender here, as usual chafing at delay, and in an agony lest the Russians should retire without fighting. In a day or two afterwards the rest of the army arrived, and all the transport animals were again sent back for provisions. Not a drop of rain had now fallen for two months, and we began to get very nervous about the continuation of the fine weather. Ominous-looking clouds gathered in the afternoons, and croakers talked about the moon changing and the weather breaking up.

Meantime we did not find the time hang heavy. We took long exploratory rides in the neighbourhood, in search of poultry and the picturesque. I had picked up an intelligent young peasant, who was in the Princess Dadian's militia, and he attached him-

self to us as interpreter, caterer, and possibly
spy.   However, he was invaluable in a commissariat point of view.   Speaking Turkish
fluently, he was also perfectly at home in Russian,
Mingrelian, Imeritian, Georgian, and Circassian,
six languages amongst the most difficult extant.
With Maxime as my guide, I used to gallop
miles away from the camp, up narrow dells,
where the houses nestle, amid thick foliage, by
the side of some brawling stream ; or over the
level country, where there was no underwood to
impede our rapid progress, and gigantic beech
and oak trees were only now beginning to drop
their yellow leaves.   One day I accompanied him
alone to his native village, which was so much
farther than usual, that I began to grow suspicious ; nor was I reassured when, on looking
at my pocket-compass, I found we were galloping straight towards the Russian outposts.   It
had not before this occurred to me that my
friend Maxime's countenance, which was singularly handsome, wore a very sinister expression.
So I suggested to him that it was time to turn
back, as it was getting late.   He at once saw
what was passing in my mind, and pointing to
my revolver, hinted, that whatever might be

his regard for me, his respect for that was unbounded. We shortly after pulled up in his
village, and the scene of our reception was
somewhat novel. Every house poured forth its
human contents as we clattered up to Maxime's
door. That young gentleman sprung from his
horse and flung himself into the arms of a series
of old hags, each one of whom caressed him in
turn, and stroked his smooth rosy cheeks with
whining expressions of admiration. Meantime
the men had been glaring so savagely at me,
that the bright glances which proceeded from
sundry other quarters scarcely reconciled me
to my position. Suddenly an old lady flung
Maxime with scorn from her bosom, and observing me, as it appeared, for the first time, heaped
upon his devoted head a torrent of vitupera-
tion so fierce and declamatory in its character,
that I could almost have supposed it to have
been in Irish instead of Mingrelian. Then rose
in wild and angry chorus the shrill voices of
all the other sisters of his grand-parents, who
went so far as to shake their fists in his face, so
that I began to fear for the poor youth's eyes.
He however behaved like a lad of spirit. Dis-
daining a reply to these withered crones, he

appealed to a patriarchal old man, who, lifting his shaking hand, stilled the tumult, and allowed Maxime to make his statement. I regret that his speech upon that occasion should not have been reported verbatim. It was delivered with immense emphasis and effect. He afterwards told me that he had appealed to their feelings of hospitality. He had brought a stranger to their village, and how had his friends and relatives received him? He was ashamed of them! —he should renounce them!—those old ladies should never see his ruddy countenance more! —his male relatives were beneath contempt, to stand there and hear his guest and friend thus insulted!! And working himself up to a pitch of virtuous indignation, with flashing eyes and heaving breast, he bade them farewell. Then one young man apologised, and as a token of submission, came to hold my stirrup when I should dismount; and another young man came threateningly forward, announcing such strong disapproval of Maxime's conduct, that my dashing young friend, whose blood was now thoroughly up, incontinently knocked him down; whereupon the old women began their vociferations afresh, and the row was going to be general, when the patriarch interposed, sent the old women grumbling away, ordered the men to be quiet, invited me to dismount and enter his house, which I immediately did, followed by the still indignant Maxime.

The grievance against Maxime was, that he had shown an infidel (as I was supposed to be) the way to so remote a village. The inhabitants not unnaturally expected that they would be visited and plundered by the whole Turkish army. Now, however, that we had a moment's tranquillity, Maxime explained that I was English, and had come to tell the people that an English army would soon appear to supersede the Turks, and that I was a Christian, and altogether a very respectable and superior sort of person. Meantime curiosity predominating over every other sentiment, female members began to drop in, and then the young men sneaked in after them, so that we had quite a levee, and I ventured to promise that their village should never again be visited—that its very existence should remain a secret. After this the men examined my Scotch shooting-boots, as being a novelty, and the women were much struck with my corduroy trousers. Then they passed round my hunting-knife with a spring, looked through my opera-glasses, were delighted with my diminutive compass, and terrified by my revolver.

After they had thoroughly examined me all over, they put some pig's head, pasta, honey, pumpkin, and sour wine on a board, round which we seated ourselves, and the conversation became general. Maxime introduced me to some very pretty sisters, while he flirted with a young lady, to see whom, I believe, was the real object of our visit. Then we smoked pipes of Mingrelian tobacco, which I found excellent. Over these we discussed politics, and the men assured me that though they hated the Turks as much as the Russians, if an English or French army came, they would be delighted to see them, and give them every assistance in the shape of supplies, &c. Whether this was genuine, or only for my benefit, I was unable to judge. Maxime now warned me that it was time to go. There was no knowing, he whispered, whether some of his enemies had not slipped off, to give intelligence to the Russian outposts, only three or four miles distant, of my visit. So after many professions of regret at their first reception of me, and of mutual goodwill, we cantered back to camp with a couple of geese and some fowls swinging from our saddles, as proofs of the success of our campaign.

I sometimes went on these expeditions without Maxime, whom I suspected of raising the price upon me ; but it was difficult to make one's wants understood. I endeavoured, therefore, to reduce the process to a system. The rules are as follows : 1st, On entering a house, when the wife shrinks into a corner, and the husband bars your entrance, produce a handful of the brightest possible sixpences ; 2d, Make the sign of the cross, and say "Anglia"—by this time you will have got inside ; 3d, Kiss the baby ; 4th, Show the pair all the curiosities of civilisation, ending with the revolver ; 5th, Point to poultry if you see any. If not, cackle or cluck, and make any sign that occurs to you for eggs, holding up sixpences—by this time. perfect confidence reigns. For general conversation, make a vocabulary on the spot, which always creates intense interest and amusement. Under all circumstances be liberal, as the news thereof may precede you to the next camping place.

My tariff was, a fowl one sixpence, a duck two, a goose three, and a turkey four. There was a good deal of competition in the matter of foraging between the few Englishmen with the army, which it was advisable to encourage, as success was always followed by a grand entertainment; and I have seldom been at more agreeable dinner-parties than, when seated round a primitive camp-table, we shared in each other's tents the spoils of these expeditions.

CHAPTER X.

In addition to what little information about their country I was enabled to gather from the Mingrelians in the course of my visits to their villages, some of the principal nobles who had been bold enough to adopt a decided line, and identify themselves with the invading army, occasionally visited our tent, and discoursed to us upon their national affairs. These men usually arrived, surrounded by their retainers, who remained grouped outside, whilst their chief was regaled within upon pipes and tea. One of them had been educated at St Petersburg, and spoke French fluently. It was singular to hear so civilised a language proceeding from the lips of a person of such uncouth exterior and wild costume ; but he was a remarkably intelligent and influential man, and his decision in compromising himself with

Russia, was significant of his confidence in the ultimate success of the Allies, and the consequent expulsion of the Russians. This poor man, together with many of his countrymen, will find their position peculiarly disagreeable if a peace with Russia restores this province to her dominions. With the exception of a few of the more intelligent natives, however, the presence of the Turkish army was decidedly unpopular.

The idea seemed firmly rooted in the minds of the inhabitants generally, that success on the part of the Turks is the inevitable precursor of permanent occupation, and they did not hesitate to admit that they dreaded such a result far more than Russian supremacy, deeming it better to bear the "ills they had than fly to others that they knew not of." They listened incredulously to any assurances to the contrary, and asked when they were to expect an English or French force, whose presence will alone relieve them from these suspicions. Thus it happened that there was no friendly feeling manifested by the people for the army. The villagers looked sullen and discontented when a party of fez - capped gentry appeared at the doors of their konaks, and were loth to supply them with anything more comforting than a cup of water or a light for a pipe ; and, so far from our stay in one place having increased their confidence generally, they probably attributed our halt to a fear of meeting the enemy, and assumed an even greater indifference to us than before.

The Mingrelians have had less reason to dislike the Muscovite rule than the inhabitants of most of the Transcaucasian provinces, because Russia has not found it either necessary or politic to subject them to the severe treatment which others more immediately in the line of her eastern progress have met with at her hands. She has deemed it wise to content herself with the right of quartering troops wherever she liked throughout the country, and the Mingrelians have benefited by the protection which was thus afforded to them from the Circassians. She has allowed the revenues of the country to flow partly into the coffers of the Dadian family, partly into those of the principal landholders and slave proprietors, reserving to herself the duties upon imports and exports, and the general control of the commercial relations of the country. Except at Redoute Kaleh she has not attempted to colonise, and, although the reigning family is completely under Russian influence, that influence is only indirectly felt by the mass of the people. These are divided into four classes : 1st, The Dadians, or reigning family, who are the proprietors of a certain number of villages, and receive from each house three dollars a-year, or a certain amount of tribute equivalent to it in kind, and the exclusive service of one member of the family, besides which they receive half-a-dollar a-year from every house in the country. 2d, The Tavit, or nobles, who own a greater or less number of villages, and receive upon the same terms as the Dadians. 3d, The Usnavors, or free men, who give military service to the Dadian, but not to the Tavit. 4th, The serfs : the latter are not exported for sale, but go, as in Russia, with the land. Over each five thousand of the inhabitants is an officer, called the Natchalnick, whose functions are to adjust disputes and administer justice. In the case of murder, the culprit is sent to Siberia ; in that of theft, the owner receives double the

amount stolen, while a fine to the same extent
is inflicted for the benefit of the Dadian.   In
addition to this, the property of all persons
dying intestate falls to the reigning prince.
He is also entitled to a certain proportion of
military service from the nobles.

Some of these perquisites are somewhat novel,
as, for instance, when a man is wounded, the
sufferer receives a pecuniary compensation in
proportion to the injury ; but the Dadian receives seventy dollars whatever it may be, so
that he gains precisely in proportion as his
subjects quarrel among themselves.   Neither
Tavits nor Usnavors sell their lands or villages
except when in embarrassed circumstances.
They then only do so with right of redemp-
tion.   They more frequently mortgage their
properties to the Dadian.   A serf can purchase
his freedom upon payment of a goat, three
pigs, some Indian corn, and wine.   He then
becomes a Usnavor ; and if he is rich enough
to buy a village, can claim the labour of a serf.

From all I could learn, the Dadianie, or
Princess, who is at present exercising the
regency, is very popular, and deservedly so,
as she pursues a most enlightened policy, and

encourages the development of the resources of the country as much as possible. She has, moreover, the merit of having out-manœuvred Russia in the matter of militia. She was asked how many militia would suffice for the defence of the country from her predatory neighbours in the Caucasus—she demanded four thousand, whom the Czar engaged to pay. She has since been receiving the annual amount necessary for that number of men, while the Mingrelian militia actually scarcely exceeds as many hundreds. Russia also engaged by treaty to protect her from foreign aggression; in this duty, however, she had now clearly failed, so that the Princess might with some show of justice submit to the new arrivals. However, treaties with Russia never seem to be of much avail to the party with whom they are contracted, and the Mingrelians have good cause to complain on more grounds than one.

It was necessary to Russia, after she had acquired Georgia, that she should possess some port upon the Black Sea. She therefore purchased the right of trading at Redoute Kaleh, and reserved to herself the privilege of levying dues, and making whatever mercantile regula-

tions she might think proper there. The re-
strictive policy which characterises her commercial relations generally, were of course
enforced here ; but the Mingrelians, who had
retained the right of doing what they pleased
at any other part on the seaboard, naturally
wished to avoid this tax upon their trade, by
choosing some other point of entry. No sooner,
however, did they attempt this, than Russia
seized their goods as contraband, and has ever
since established a preventive service to obstruct
the prosecution of that free commerce, to the enjoyment of which they have a perfect right. The
spirit of the population is thoroughly mercantile,
and they desire nothing more earnestly than
to assist in developing resources probably not
surpassed in extent and variety by any country
in the world. Almost the sole use which is
at present made of the only navigable river in
the province, the Rhion, is as a means of carrying so-called *contraband* goods into the interior.
The boats which navigate the river draw five feet
of water, and carry eighteen hundred okes of
grain : they ascend to Mehranie, about fifteen
miles from Kutais. It is to be hoped that one
of the results of this war may be to have justice

K

done to the Mingrelians in this matter, and to throw open the province to commercial enterprise.

With the exception of a battalion quartered at Redoute Kaleh in time of peace, there are no Russian troops stationed in Mingrelia. Altogether, it is fair to say that the people generally gave me the impression of being happy and contented, though whether they are destined always to remain so, is another matter.

It was a pleasant ride to Skender's camp, five miles in advance, situated upon the river Techoua. From hence Ferhad Pasha had pushed a reconnaissance as far as the Skeniscal, where he had a slight skirmish with the outposts of the Russians, who had gradually retired until they had placed this river between themselves and their enemy. The Turks succeeded in surrounding some Cossacks, of whom they killed one and made two prisoners. One object of the expedition was to induce the inhabitants to rebuild the bridges which they had destroyed. While visiting one of the villages the General had a narrow escape : he was accompanied by a few irregular Circassian horsemen, who had replaced

the Abkhasians, but whose predatory tendencies were in every respect the same, and even
more strongly developed. As soon as the villagers saw the arrival of these dreaded mountaineers, they assembled to defend their homes
and families ; and making no doubt of the
object of their visit, were about to commence
the assault, when the Circassians, seeing they
would be outnumbered, took to their heels,
leaving Ferhad Pasha and his aide-de-camp to
get out of the scrape as best they could. It
was with considerable difficulty that they succeeded in effecting their escape.

These Circassians, whose functions were to
hover about our line of march, and keep us
informed of the enemy's proceedings, were
really utterly useless, and did infinite mischief in terrifying the people, and predisposing them against us. I was more than
once an eyewitness of their violence. On
one occasion I accompanied Colonel Caddell
upon an expedition to Sinakia, a town about
two miles from Skender's camp, where a few
adventurous inhabitants had brought luxuries
for sale ; for Sinakia was, after Sugdidi, the
most considerable place in Mingrelia. While

engaged in buying English bottled stout at seven shillings a bottle, and sardines at five shillings a tin, we heard shrieks arising from the woods behind us so loud and piercing, that if I had been in England I should have supposed myself in the neighbourhood of a tunnel at which three express trains were all arriving at the same moment, and informing one another of the fact. The street, which had been thickly sprinkled with country people, became deserted in an instant, and the whole population rushed towards the spot. Caddell and I jumped upon our horses, and, passing the panting crowd, arrived first at the village, to which we were guided by the cries of women and the sterner shouts of men, when a strange scene met our eyes. Brandishing flails, fence-sticks, and whatever other weapon they could find, a multitude of women and a few old men were offering a stout resistance to some twenty or thirty Circassians, a few of whom had dismounted from their horses with the evident intention of effecting a forcible entry. They had reckoned upon the young men being at Sinakia to accomplish this with impunity; but they had miscalculated the power of lung of the female part of the community, and now to their astonishment they saw us both ride furiously up, with indignation rather more strongly expressed in our countenances than Turkish officers (which we were supposed to be) usually display. Active hostilities were about to commence, as the young men came rushing to the conflict ; but we managed to keep them back, and ordered the Circassians to decamp. This command they were by no means disposed to obey. "These are Giaours," they said ; "they eat pig" (as if this justified any barbarity). "You are Giaours," cried Caddell, indignantly. "*I* am a Giaour," I bawled out ; "and what's more, I delight in pork !" This was a startling announcement, and they seemed more inclined to resist than ever the authority of two unknown Christians. "We'll report you to the commander-in-chief, you plundering blackguards," said Caddell, riding threateningly into the middle of them with uplifted hunting-whip. "But I am a mighty Bey," replied a red ruffian, whose coat, and beard, and kalpak were all the same colour. "Then give me your name," said I, taking out my note-book, solemnly. This was too much ; they could stand any amount of abuse, or even cold steel, but there is something mysterious about a note-book and pencil which strikes terror into the heart of a savage. So off trooped the party, leaving us to receive the benedictions of the whole population, who clustered round to kiss our legs; while the old ladies, who are peculiarly demonstrative in Mingrelia, flung out their arms and clasped them together, thus pressing us in imagination to their withered bosoms.

Finding that the Circassians had not returned to the high-road, we galloped to Skender to tell him what had occurred. He said he had done his utmost to prevent it; had himself ordered the red-bearded Bey not to plunder; and that the red-bearded Bey had replied to him, as he did to us, that he was a mighty Bey; and he added that he would do exactly what he liked, and if Skender tried to prevent him, he would shoot him. Whereupon Skender replied that he also would do what he liked; and to the astonishment of that great gentleman, and the amazement of his retainers, Skender ordered him there and then to be lashed down at the door of his tent, and the usual functionary of the battalion was forthwith enjoined to give him a round three dozen, which were laid on without sparing, as Skender remarked to him, " To improve your shooting, mighty Bey !" It was some consolation to know that this latter incident had occurred, and it accounted for the unwillingness of this red-bearded gentleman to favour us with his name.

I was afterwards deterred from making any complaint to Omer upon the subject, as I heard that he had given orders that the Circassians should not be prevented from stealing *a little*. As they received neither pay nor rations, it was rather difficult to limit the amount.

One morning a spy was brought into camp in Mingrelian costume, who turned out to be an aide-de-camp of the Russian General Mock-ransky. As soon as his identity was indisputably proved by the evidence of some of the chiefs and country people who knew him, Omer Pasha ordered him to be shot. The unfortunate man met his fate with the utmost composure, expressing his innocence to the last. I afterwards met his body, preceded by a priest in full canonicals, on its way to receive Christian burial.

The priests were, as usual, to a certain extent, an intelligent class ; and in the course of my rides I occasionally visited those monasteries upon the tops of the hills, which they had not deserted.   Sinakia was, however, the most popular resort with us, as being a comparatively near approach to civilisation.   It was composed of two streets of wooden houses, and had been deserted upon our approach, the inhabitants taking refuge in the woods, bearing with them thither all their stock in trade.   When, however, our harmless character and readiness to pay fabulous prices was discovered, five or six storekeepers returned and opened their shops, in which a few of the luxuries of civilisation could be procured : though the wine was undrinkable, both English bottled stout and Russian vodka were acceptable.   The town was situated at the base of a range of hills, about two thousand feet high, upon a spur of which had been perched the picturesque old castle of Schchekheppe, with its unpronounceable name and heavy tower, rising, in the form of a truncated cone, above its massive walls covered with ivy.   It was the residence formerly of one of the Dadians, and still belongs to one of them. There were two or three spacious mansions, evidently belonging to Beys of importance, who had deserted them. In one a regiment of Skender's division was located. That gallant old officer was busily employed in constructing a bridge over the Techoua, which, though now low, in the event of rain would present a formidable obstacle to our progress.

At last the long-expected rain did come, and the first thing it did was to carry away poor Skender's bridge; the next, to sweep down the bridge which had been constructed across the Ziewie, and to cut off all communication between one half of the camp and the other. That placid river was now a seething torrent; it rose about fourteen feet in one night, and the waterfall consequently disappeared. After that it continued to rise, until I thought the old ruin on the island would give way at last; but it stopped, and gradually subsided. Not so the rain—that was incessant; and to our disgust, we discovered that in the centre of our tent, which was pitched upon the side of a hill, there was a spring; so we were fairly flooded out, and had to move to

another piece of sloppy ground higher up.   We
waited in despair for the rain to cease, and for
Skender to build another bridge.   This he at
last succeeded in accomplishing, though it was
only available for foot-passengers ; and upon
the morning of the 2d of December, in the
middle of a tremendous storm, the army
received the order to march.

CHAPTER XI.

WE were not sorry at last to leave the banks of the Ziewie, upon which we had spent a fort-night of most precious time, and only regretted that our day's march terminated at Sinakia. The Rifles were more highly favoured than any other corps in the army, for we were quartered in the town. The inhabitants, after divesting their houses of their contents, had locked the doors and taken away the keys ; so nothing remained for us but to smash the padlocks. For an hour after our entry there was a universal hammering and appropriation of houses going on, in which the men much delighted. While their comrades were out pitching their tents in a pitiless storm, they were warmly sheltered, and soon engaged in cooking, and drying them-selves by the side of cheerful fires, after their wet day's march. Ballard and I got into an

excellent wooden house, with two little store-
rooms opening upon one of the verandas,
which formed the footway on each side of the
street ; at the back of these was a large boarded
room, in the centre of which a square space was
left and paved with stone to serve as a fire-
place ; the smoke found its own way out
through chinks in the roof. We discovered
two wooden stretchers here, and revelled in
the luxury of dining and sleeping, like civilised
beings, in a house.

On the following morning we were *en route*
at daylight. The great business of crossing the
swollen Techoua was to be accomplished ; and
when we arrived at the bank, a scene of confusion presented itself which at once convinced us
that the task was to be by no means an easy
one. The whole army was assembled upon the
plain, which was at an elevation of about
seventy feet above the river, and knee-deep in
mud. Aides-de-camp were galloping, soldiers
were wading, guns were sticking, and baggage-
horses rolling in the mire. Below us swept
the turbid stream, about fifty yards in breadth,
and at this point unfordable. Across it a
narrow and very fragile-looking foot-bridge

had been placed, while below it a ferry, constructed of two pontoons, was making an experimental trip across.

The soldiers now began in single file to pass the trembling bridge, and form on the other side. The guns were carefully let down the bank, and, with much difficulty, placed upon the ferry; but from the time occupied in this operation, and in the traject of the men, it was clear that many hours must elapse before the whole army would be collected upon the other side. It was most fortunate, then, that a ford was discovered lower down, and long lines of cavalry, infantry, and artillery, were soon after seen following one another into the rapid current. The water reached up to the waists of the men. After I had forded, I turned to sketch the scene; it was one worth remembering. At three different points the army was crossing the river, at each in a different method, whilst on the bank above a group of horsemen were assembled, whose more brilliant uniforms denoted the presence of the Commander-in-Chief superintending operations. The picturesque old castle I have before named crowned one of the hills

in the background, whilst the lofty range closed
the prospect.   Upon looking through my
glass at the summit of one of these hills, I observed a group of persons who were evidently
watching us, and on a closer inspection I discovered their lances.   They were pronounced
to be the enemy's irregular cavalry ; and upon
the fact being announced to Omer, he immediately sent a party of Circassians to reconnoitre.
The leader of the party afterwards reported that,
upon approaching the spot, he concealed his
men, and proceeded alone to reconnoitre.   Upon
being discovered, he was fired upon, and his
Circassians then charging, the Georgian militia
fled down the opposite side of the hill and
escaped.

Meantime the discovery of the ford had
materially expedited matters generally, and
shortly after mid-day the whole army was on
the march.   The weather, though threatening,
remained fine, and we pushed on until the darkness compelled us to camp near a small stream,
where the bridge which the country-people had
erected had been washed away.   The previous
rains had made camping by no means so agreeable as formerly, and we pitched our tents in a

muddy field of Indian-corn stubble. The next
morning saw us again *en route*. The road was
literally knee-deep in mud, so that we preferred scrambling through the woods and over
the corn-fields to following it. Every mile, or
even less, there was a deep stream to cross,
which always created a good deal of delay. One
of these, the Abasha, was almost as formidable
as the Techoua, and I looked forward with some
apprehension to the Skeniscal, which was reported to be a great deal larger than either.
However, the weather still continued fine, and
we hoped that the waters would have subsided
sufficiently to admit of our effecting the passage.

We camped at a distance of about two miles
from the Skeniscal ; and being now again in the
presence of the enemy, care was required in
placing the outposts. I rode round them
with the Sirdar Ekrem (Omer Pasha) in
the afternoon, and he cheered the hearts
of the men as he passed, by telling them
that on the following day they should fight
the Russians. They answered with loud shouts
of " Inshallah !" Intelligence had indeed arrived that, although not prepared to dispute
the passage of the river, the enemy had taken

up a position near Mehranie, about two miles
from it, where they intended to risk another
general action.   We had little doubt as to the
results ; and as we were also informed that the
river had so far subsided as to become fordable, we were sanguine that the following day
would see a victory even more brilliant than
the Ingour, and would be followed a few hours
after by the capture of Kutais.   It was also
said that Bebutoff, who had been despatched
by Mouravieff to take the command, had arrived with considerable reinforcements.   Full of
confidence that the campaign, after all, was to
be crowned with success, we returned towards
camp, but had scarce done so when a few large
drops of rain damped at once our jackets and
our hopes.   All that night it poured incessantly ;
never, except in the tropics, and even rarely
there, have I witnessed so determined a deluge.
It seemed impossible that any tent could resist
it, and consequently, after standing out bravely
for some time, ours began at last to let it in by
drops.   Under these circumstances it was not
to be wondered at that our slumbers should be
light, and we jumped from our damp beds
without regret when a rattle of small-arms

close to us, a little before dawn, informed us that the weather had not deterred the enemy from attempting a surprise. The camp was under arms without a moment's delay, and as the outposts engaged had belonged to our corps, I galloped with Ballard to see what was going on. Before we arrived, the firing had ceased, and the enemy had retired. This alarm, however, suggested, notwithstanding the continued violence of the weather, the propriety of a reconnaissance; and accordingly, after breakfast, we made an exploration, with two battalions of Rifles, in the direction from which the attack had been made. We saw the prints of many hoofs, but it was clear that the enemy had retired, though, from the flooded state of the country, it was highly improbable that they could have recrossed the river. They had evidently consisted only of cavalry.

This reconnaissance was made with the utmost difficulty. Every ditch was swollen, and the whole country was intersected by rapid deep streams, quite unfordable for infantry. A great part of it was absolutely under water. Some idea of the rapidity with which these floods had risen, may be formed from the fact

L

that the stream which separated our tent from
Omer Pasha's, and which, the day before, had
scarcely reached up to the horses' knees, was
now quite unfordable either for man or beast.   I
returned from our expedition in a miserable
plight, for in jumping a ditch my horse fell
back with me into about eight feet of water.
As there was no possibility of making a fire,
my clothes remained wet for many days afterwards.

The next day I accompanied another reconnaissance, which had for its object the thorough
exploration of the river.   Colonel Simmons
and Ballard went down stream : I followed
Skender Pasha in the opposite direction.   It
still rained without intermission ; but as we
started wet through from camp, that did not
much signify.   Our first view of the river did
not tend to reassure us.   It was at least two
hundred yards broad, and rushed down with a
fury nothing could withstand.   Forest trees
were tossing upon its boiling surface—islands
of vegetable matter were being swept along it—
the topmost branches of submerged trees bent
to the flood—and portions of the bank where
we were standing, undermined by its violence,

at intervals fell in and disappeared. It seemed scarcely necessary to explore further; but Skender was loth to give up hope, so we rode for five or six miles along the bank. Now and then we could see the figures of the Russian soldiers posted upon the opposite side, but they did not fire at us. The country-people showed us a number of places where the river was fordable in fair weather, but they laughed at the idea of attempting to cross it in its present state; so we turned reluctantly back, after being so near Kutais that, had we been on the other side of the stream, in two hours' smart riding we should have reached it.

On our way back we stopped at the villages through which we passed, as Skender delighted in pulling up in the rain to talk to the inhabitants. I was struck with the gradual change in the appearance both of the people and of the country since we had first entered Mingrelia. There was scarcely a trace of that lawless character which distinguishes those upon the frontier of Abkhasia. The people were universally unarmed. The tall pointed kalpak or headdress was here replaced by a singular flat piece of cloth, which looked exactly like a kettle-holder, and which, only covering the top of the head, was fastened under the chin, and allowed a profusion of black hair to fall over the back of the neck and shoulders. These men showed considerable alarm at our appearance, which was in a great measure due to the consciousness that they deserved correction. Every road had been carefully blocked up by trees felled across it, and Skender pointed indignantly to the obstacles which had thus been placed in our way. The excuse we received from the peasants was, that they had been coerced by the Russians. The cultivation in the neighbourhood of the villages was of a much more civilised character than I had before seen. Neat fences enclosed the fields and bordered the roads; while the houses, still of wood, were more elaborately constructed, and substantial in appearance. In fact, the aspect of the people and of the country was more advanced and prosperous, although, when we asked for supplies, we received the usual answer, that the Russians had cleared the country of everything it contained.

Upon reaching the camp I found that Ballard had returned from his reconnaissance. They had explored the river with as little success as we had, and perceived large bodies of the enemy. These had opened a fire upon our men, but not being replied to, they contented themselves with watching their proceedings and taking off their hats to them ; no doubt chuckling over their fruitless endeavours to discover a passage by which to cross over, and return the compliment at closer quarters.

CHAPTER XII.

THE incessant rains had by this time reduced our camp to a deplorable state. The level plain upon which it was pitched was absolutely under water, and no amount of trenching was sufficient to prevent the floors of the tents from being flooded. Our next neighbour, Omer Bey, Colonel Ballard's aide-de-camp, called me to witness a forcible illustration of our semi-drowned condition. He had made prize of a duck in the course of a foraging expedition, which he had tethered inside his tent. It had got away from its string, and was now actually swimming by the bedside of its owner, gobbling up bits of floating biscuit. The condition of the unfortunate soldiers under these circumstances may easily be conceived. Crowded into their small tents, they lay literally packed in mud. My own bed was upon the ground, or rather in the water, and for the last two nights I had been suffering from fever and ague. To add to our miseries, we were running short of provisions. Our horses, which had been exposed to the rain without the slightest shelter, began to look careworn and miserable; nor was the appearance of the men more cheering. The Rifles had been incessantly at work. When not marching, they were employed in reconnaissances; and I do not believe that a more enduring body of men exist anywhere than these gallant fellows proved themselves to be. No doubt, a great deal was due to the care which their commanding officer took to keep their commissariat well supplied. Had they fared as badly as many of the other regiments, they certainly could never have gone through their work. Some of their less fortunate comrades had already been out of provisions altogether, and came to buy from the Rifles biscuits at ten paras a-piece.

Such was the state of the army when, upon the morning of the 8th December, the weather showing no signs of improvement, the order came for retreat. Although we were fully alive to the obstacles which opposed themselves to

our advance, still the order took us completely
by surprise, and we could scarcely realise the
disagreeable truth that we were about to give up
all hopes of another battle, all chances of reaching Kutais ; and, turning our backs upon the
enemy, begin a toilsome and dispiriting tramp
over the many weary miles of mud we had
already traversed.   Still it was perfectly clear
that no other course remained open to us.   The
rivers in rear were rising, and already cut off
communication with our depôts at Ziewie.
There was only a certain amount of provision
remaining in camp, and that was barely sufficient to enable us to return.   The Rifles and
some of the other corps had, it is true, a few
days' extra provisions, but that was of little
avail.   The fact that this was so, was to be
attributed entirely to the judicious arrangements of the officers commanding.   There is
no commissariat corps in the Turkish as in our
army, but each regiment is supplied with a
certain number of commissariat animals.   By
sometimes leaving his tents behind for a day
or two, Ballard was enabled to avail himself of
the service of the transport as well as of the
bât animals.   He thus stole a march upon the

rest of the army. The reason given for our fortnight's detention at Ziewie, was the necessity of forming depôts there, because it was alleged that we had not animals enough to bring our provisions to a greater distance from the coast. Whether so large a depôt was necessary, or whether the whole operation might not have been effected in a shorter time, I cannot say; but one thing is certain, that with three times the number of transport animals we should have been in Kutais a fortnight before this time. When it is remembered that our land-transport corps in the Crimea contains twenty-two thousand horses, it will, I think, be admitted that two thousand animals were scarcely sufficient for an army of nearly thirty thousand men.

As soon as it was known that we were to retreat, the greatest disappointment was manifested everywhere : the men declared they would rather perish in the river before them than turn back. What made the matter more provoking, was our knowledge of the fact that boats were lying at Redoute Kaleh, ready loaded to ascend the Rhion, so that if we could have got across the Skeniscal we should not only have beat the Russians, but have been enabled to receive our supplies by water direct all the way from our base of operations, and our commissariat difficulties would have been at an end. We all turned out of our sloppy beds to allow our tents to be struck, and stood, drooping and miserable, up to our knees in mud and water. As the Rifles were to form the rearguard, they were condemned to wait, exposed to the rain, until the whole army was on the march. At last I could bear it no longer, and, leaving Ballard and his men to the exercise of patient resignation, I galloped towards the front. The stream which I was obliged to cross had not subsided, and swept my horse off his legs, so we had to swim for it. A little higher up they were busily engaged in making a bridge. I found that Omer and his staff had disappeared; and learning from Osman Pasha that the Rifles were to camp on the ground he had just vacated, I took eager possession of a deserted house, and promised myself, at all events, the comfort of a fire and a dry floor. I also heard, for the first time, the news, which had arrived the evening before, of the fall of Kars. Though I had never thought

HERR ZUTHER, DEL.

M & N HANHART, IMP

HEAD QUARTERS OF OMER PACHA, NEAR THE SKENISCAL.

1

it possible, at so late a period of the year, to relieve it, yet it was doubly annoying to think that we should not now have made any equivalent conquest to set off against the Russian success. I do not think that the intelligence could have influenced Omer Pasha in deciding upon a retreat, as, in the first place, the natural obstacles which impeded his progress put any advance out of the question; and, in the second, the results of success, apart from the salvation of Kars, would have been such as to warrant his straining every nerve to achieve it.

The functions of the rearguard of an army during a retreat may be very honourable, but they are by no means agreeable. We were always under arms before anybody else, and did not get under canvass until after our neighbours were snug. We travelled over a road rendered almost impassable by the double journey of thirty thousand men, at the rate of a mile an hour. Every few yards there was a stoppage, generally originating in the artillery. It reminded me very much of being in the last carriage of the file when going to the opera, upon a wet night; only, instead of being inside a carriage, I was what is vulgarly called " out-

side a horse ;" and instead of the misery last-
ing for only half-an-hour, and being amply
compensated for by comfort and entertainment
afterwards, it lasted for the whole day, and was
succeeded at night by the pleasures of a tent
like a shower-bath, and a bed in the mud.

There was an immense deal of confusion
upon the march. If Turkish pashas are averse
to advancing, they certainly do not show the
same antipathy to retreating, and leaving their
men to find their own way. They invariably
keep well ahead ; the consequence is an utter
absence of order just when it is most necessary. At one period of our day's march, upon
arriving on the banks of the Abasha, the confusion was so great that five hundred Cossacks
might have done us infinite mischief with comparative impunity. We were just camping
upon a plain partially covered with water, when
Skender, who had been engaged in frantic
endeavours to restore order, arrived, and asked
for two companies of Rifles to make a reconnaissance, under the command of one of his
aides-de-camp, Mehemet Ali Effendi. We had
been on so many fruitless expeditions of this
nature, and were so much knocked up by cold

and wet, that neither Ballard nor I felt disposed to accompany him ; so we discussed our last bottle of port with Skender, and grumbled over the aspect of things in general.

The Pasha had scarcely left the tent when a pretty smart fire of musketry informed us that the small party under Mehemet Ali had got into a mess, and required support. The order was immediately given for four companies of Rifles to get under arms.

Whilst our horses were being saddled, I observed, flying over the plain, two singularly accoutred equestrians : the leading one, mounted upon a magnificent Arab, covered with gorgeous trappings, was a swarthy figure, whose nondescript costume bore more resemblance to that of a Bedouin Arab than to that of a Turkish officer. Waving his rifle above his head, he dashed straight across the country in the direction from whence the firing proceeded. His follower was a negro, mounted upon an inferior animal, which he nevertheless urged at its utmost pace, while he, too, flourished his gun above his turban. Three or four magnificent Persian greyhounds followed with graceful stride, and completed the picturesque group,

whose sudden appearance at this stage of affairs
puzzled me not a little, as I had never before
observed them during the campaign.   We soon
after followed in the same direction, at a more
sober pace, and after marching for about a
mile, reached the scene of action.   Concealing
his men behind some thick brushwood, Ballard
and I rode on to inspect more closely the state
of affairs.

We found the Rifles retreating before about
five hundred mounted Georgians, who kept
at pretty long range, but were nevertheless
maintaining an incessant but harmless fire,
in answer to the sharp ping of our rifles.
The Arab and his servant held a conspicuous
position : dashing out of our own ranks, they
approached to within a few yards of the enemy,
loading and firing, without taking the slightest
notice of the fire which was being concentrated
upon them.   As soon as Ballard saw the position of affairs, he gave the order for a hasty
retreat, hoping thereby to lure the enemy into
the ambush he had prepared for them.   They,
however, had in the mean time sent some skirmishers to our rear, apparently with the design
of surrounding us, when, finding the reception

we had prepared for them, they precipitately drew off, having lost altogether about twelve men. There was no casualty on the side of the Turks, although I observe in the Russian official account of this skirmish, which was magnified into a victory, the officer commanding reports our loss in killed and wounded to have been very great.

My first inquiry, upon our return home, was regarding the Arab gentleman, who had found amusement in getting into the line of fire of both parties, and who was now gaily caracoling back to camp, followed by his negro and his greyhounds. I was informed that he was none other than Bou Maza, the celebrated lieutenant of Abd-el-Kader, who had attained the rank of colonel in the Turkish army, and who, lacking the excitement of his wild life in Algeria, had come to seek it as an amateur in Mingrelia.

At daylight next morning our tents were struck, and we had the disagreeable duty to perform of protecting the passage of the Abasha. We were the last to cross, and had no sooner reached the opposite bank than we observed the Cossacks appearing upon the

plain which had formed our last night's camping-ground. Seeing that they were determined
to hover as closely as possible upon our rear,
we formed sundry little traps for them, hiding
the Rifles in the bushes. But they were as shy as
grouse in October, and only once came within
shot. This day's march was even more disagreeable than the last. Numerous horses lying
dead by the road-side showed that the work
was beginning to tell ; while many of the men
were so knocked up with fatigue and starvation that they could scarcely crawl along. It
rained, as usual, incessantly, and the Techoua
was even more flooded than when we had
crossed it last. However, we managed to encamp on the opposite bank before dark.

During the night I heard a few stray shots ;
and next morning, when I rode up to see Omer
Pasha for the first time since our retreat, he
told me that a sentry had been shot. He also
said that he had good reason to know that the
country-people were assisting the enemy by
every means in their power, and expressed his
determination to deal with them accordingly.
He seemed, not unnaturally, in low spirits at
the unfortunate issue of the campaign, in which

his usual luck seemed to have deserted him. Upon returning to my tent, I found myself suffering from a complication of diseases, of which ague and rheumatism were the most trifling; so I incontinently ensconced myself between my wet blankets, and tried to shed off the rain as it dropped through the tent, by making a sort of awning of my waterproof sheet. I was consequently too much taken up with my own miseries to accompany Ballard and a party of his men in the direction of Sinakia, where some firing had been heard; but before nightfall he sent his aide-de-camp to move the whole corps up to that town, where I was glad once more to install myself in our old quarters.

It appeared that a skirmish had taken place in the streets of the town between the Circassians and Georgians, in which a man was killed on each side. Upon the appearance of the Rifles, the Georgians as usual retired. The town was now completely deserted. The few adventurous shopkeepers had scarcely found time to make their escape before it had become a scene of bloodshed. We had sent a servant in the morning to make some purchases; he

M

saw no one in the town but a Turkish corporal, apparently bound upon a similar mission ;
but fearing, from its deserted aspect, that the
enemy might be near, he returned with all
speed to camp—as it turned out, just in time,
for the Circassians whom he met found the
Georgians in the town. The headless trunk
of the unfortunate corporal was discovered in
a house just opposite ours, the Georgians having thus barbarously mutilated the body. A
baggage-horse of mine, which had preceded
me, happened to be standing near at the
time, and I was astonished, upon riding into
the town, to meet him returning with so un-
sightly a burden, as the poor man was being
borne back to the regiment to which he had
belonged.

CHAPTER XIII.

As no obligation lay upon me to link my fortunes any longer with the Rifles, and as no glory, but a great deal of discomfort, was gained by remaining with them, I determined to follow the example of Omer Pasha, and push ahead as rapidly as possible.   I was indebted to Colonel Caddell for a night's lodging at our old camp on the banks of the Ziewie, where I also met Mr Longworth.   During the night we heard some dropping shots, and next morning discovered that two sentries had been shot within thirty yards of the doctors' tents. The proximity of these guerilla horsemen was disagreeable in more ways than one : not only did one go to sleep with a feeling of great insecurity, but our foraging expeditions were completely put an end to, and meat was in consequence an unknown luxury.   We were

dependent entirely upon supplies, consisting
only of rice and biscuit, brought up from
Redoute Kaleh, along twenty-five miles of
almost impassable road, and by animals so
weak, that latterly not much more than half
of those who started ever reached their destination.

In the way of drinkables, we were reduced
to water, and some very bad tea which we
procured at Sinakia.   Even our stock of
tobacco was exhausted ; and we were thus
deprived of the ordinary consolations in seasons of hardship and exposure, and of all
stimulants or nourishing diet, rendered doubly
necessary by the sickness from which most of
us were suffering.

From Ziewie I rode on with Mr Longworth
to the headquarters of Omer Pasha, and found
them prettily situated at the top of a gentle
eminence near the monastery of Choloni.   Here
it was determined that the army should go into
winter-quarters, as the formation of the country
afforded great natural advantages of position.

Our arrival was commemorated by a gleam
of sunshine, which was unspeakably comforting, as it not only helped to dry my clothes,

but to relieve my mind of an apprehension which I had begun to entertain, that that luminary never intended to favour us with his presence again.

While enjoying this delightful novelty, and looking over the magnificent view presented by the valley of the Rhion, lying between lofty snow-covered ranges, my attention was arrested by loud and dismal cries, which I observed to proceed from a procession of natives, who were coming down the slope of an opposite hill. As they approached, I saw it was a funeral, and that the steps of the mourners were directed towards the burial-ground near which I was then standing. As they drew closer, the shrill wailing of the women became more piercing and discordant, and attracted a number of Turks, who eyed with cynical looks the ceremony of a Christian burial. The women tore their hair, faces, and breasts ; in some cases they had frightfully lacerated themselves ; and blood was trickling down their cheeks and bosoms. All the time that they stood round the grave, they continued thus to demonstrate their grief for the departed, while an old priest came out to superintend operations, and mutter a prayer; but I did not see him read any service.

The men were a long time letting down the coffin and covering in the grave, so I went into the church to see if there was any ceremony being performed there. From this, however, I was speedily ejected by another door, and found myself in an open veranda, in the presence of a lady in the guise of a tragedy queen: a magnificent tunic of green velvet, trimmed with fur, fell gracefully over a rich silk dress, while a head-dress of silver brocade completed her gorgeous costume. She was in close confabulation with a gentleman, whose high-peaked hat, short jacket, and gaiters, gave him rather the appearance of an Italian brigand. Two or three female attendants were standing near, elegantly dressed in the costume of the country; while an imposing group of armed Mingrelians, who stood at a more respectful distance, had evidently formed her escort. Just as I was wondering who this Mingrelian dame could be, Omer Pasha's band, encouraged by the fine weather, struck up an air from Norma; and as if to invest the scene with a still more theatrical effect, the gentleman,

HERR ZUTHER DEL.   M.&N. HANHART, IMP.

INTERVIEW BETWEEN OMER PACHA & A MINGRELIAN LADY.—HEAD QUARTERS, CHOLONI.

ately to be fear   Prin
  appropriated to

offering his hand to the lady, led her, with slow and stately step, through the ruined archway in the old wall which encompassed the monastery, into the presence of Omer Pasha, who, enveloped in a yellow robe, was seated, *en vrai Turque*, at the door of a wooden cottage, in which he had established his quarters. The lady was received with a great deal of ceremony, and, entering the house, vanished from the stage, followed by the General.

The mysterious lady, as I afterwards heard, was a friend of the Princess Dadianie's, who had come down to Omer Pasha to make a complaint with reference to the conduct of Prince Michael, who, it appeared, had turned the battle of the Ingour to good account. The island on which the action had taken place, had long been a subject of dispute between the princes of Mingrelia and those of Abkhasia ; it formed part of that district of Samoursachan, the revenues of which, as I have before said, Russia has hitherto transferred to her own coffers, in order to prevent the quarrels of the rival claimants. Now, however, that neither Russia nor Mingrelia were immediately to be feared, Prince Michael very wisely appropriated to himself

260 families, together with their goods and chattels, who had formerly inhabited the island ; and this lady was an emissary sent by the Dadianie to seek redress. Her claim to this was very. properly not recognised by Omer, as it might have been had she appeared herself to prefer her complaint. The lady consequently departed without satisfaction ; but I was fortunate enough to make the acquaintance of the gentleman. He was the Comte de Rosmorduc, a French gentleman who had settled in Sugdidi twenty years previously : he had since been engaged in manufacturing silk with considerable success, and was an intimate personal friend and adviser of the Dadianie's.

Although the Princess has always been treated with the utmost consideration by Russia, there can be no doubt that she would earnestly desire to be rendered altogether independent of that power, and thereby be enabled to develop the resources of her country, and advance, by a more enlightened policy than that uniformly pursued by Russia, its material interests. She sees before her that inevitable destiny which has already overtaken other of the Transcaucasian provinces, where the line of the reigning princes has become extinct, and the nobles have dwindled into third-class Russian officials. Thus it happens, that as the process of incorporation of a province into the Muscovite empire gradually progresses, the unpopularity of Russian rule becomes more widely and deeply felt. The different stages of absorption are singularly exemplified in Transcaucasia. Georgia, the administration of whose affairs is entirely in the hands of Russian officials, is to all intents and purposes a Russian province. The nobles, indeed, occasionally receive large pensions ; but as the revenue of the country is monopolised by Russia, the power of the nobles over the peasantry no longer exists ; whilst, as the price of living is enhanced by the introduction of foreign luxuries, they are in reality poorer than they were before. Some go into government offices, and are made use of as revenue collectors in districts where it would not be safe for Russians to appear. Amongst the Tavats, who have in a great measure lost, under the Muscovite regime, that position in the community which the constitution of their own society formerly allowed them, the rule of Russia is no less unpopular ; whilst the differences which exist between the Georgian and the Russian Greek religions afford fruitful sources of jealousy and dislike.

The government of Imeritia is, practically, exclusively Russian ; but there is a semblance of power vested in the hands of four of the principal nobles of the country, who meet in council at Kutais for the purpose of advising with the governor, and of exercising certain administrative and judicial functions. The natchalniks, or local officers, are appointed by Russia. The population of Imeritia numbers about two hundred thousand.

In Gouriel, a province lying between Mingrelia and Turkey, Russia has ever found it a difficult task to assert her supremacy. Consisting of a series of impracticable mountain-chains, the Mussulman population who inhabit it have been enabled to take advantage of the nature of their country to resist the Russian dominion, to which they have always manifested the liveliest aversion. Had their country been more accessible, there can be no doubt that a Turkish army, advancing through it upon Kutais, would have found that the sympathies of the country-people were in their favour.

The principal family in Gouriel is the Data, who are connected with the Dadians. Indeed, Prince Gregoire Dadian's wife is the next in succession of the Data family : considering, however, the conduct of this gentleman, who was at that moment commanding those guerilla horsemen who were hovering upon our line of march, it is to be hoped that, in the event of Russia ever being deprived of that province, it would not fall into the hands of one so devoted to her interests. Ouzourgeth is the capital of the province, and a station at which Russian troops are constantly posted.

The relative position of Mingrelia with Russia I have already described. The province contains a population of about eighty-five thousand inhabitants. If the people here have not imbibed that aversion to her rule which those who have been brought directly under it have invariably manifested, it is because they are as yet ignorant of its crushing and fatal influences, and lack that spirit of independence which has been powerful enough in Abkhasia to limit the power of Russian aggression, and in Circassia altogether to defy it.

Perhaps, however, the true secret of the comparatively tranquil condition of these provinces is to be found in the enlightened policy of Prince Woronzoff, whose long and eminently success- ful administration has been so efficacious in reconciling the people to the Muscovite yoke, in improving their material condition, and in developing the internal resources of the country, that these provinces cannot be taken as a fair sample of Russian administration, but rather as a proof of the beneficial effects of a system of government of which, in Russia, Prince Woronzoff is the only exponent. Had it not been for that eminent statesman, the sym- pathies of the populations of these provinces would have been in our favour to a tenfold greater extent than they are ; and a military force would have been devoted to their defence, which would have rendered any such campaign as that in which we were now engaged im- practicable, and would have secured, beyond a doubt, these provinces against any danger of conquest. In consequence of those troops not having been sent to him which Prince Woron- zoff deemed necessary for this purpose, he re- signed his government.

Monsieur de Rosmorduc had joined the

army upon the advance, having fled with the Princess Dadianie to Gordi after the battle of the Ingour. As the success of the Turkish arms became apparently more inevitable, the Princess retired to her still more inaccessible fortress of Muri, where Monsieur de Rosmorduc had left her to join the Turkish army, and doubtless to pave the way for her adhesion. The retreat, however, effected an entire alteration in the Princess's plans, and it was not to be wondered at that she should subsequently have abstained from compromising herself. Muri was described as a stronghold at so great an elevation in the mountains, that when Monsieur de Rosmorduc left it, the snow lay upon the ground to the depth of three or four feet.

The road thither is so perilous that it can be reached on horseback only with the utmost difficulty. By ascending the same valley in which Muri is situated, the explorer of these almost unknown regions arrives at the country of Swaneth, which had not been visited by any stranger previously to Monsieur de Rosmorduc. He describes them as a wild and fierce people, Pagans in their religion, and evincing the strongest suspicion of Europeans. No Russian dares enter within the limits of their country. Their houses are large sheds partitioned off into stalls, and capable of containing fifty or sixty persons. He mentioned numerous Italian names as being common amongst them. Farther east is the country of the Ossetæ, inhabited by a still more savage race, whose language bears a strong resemblance to German.

Circassian.

CHAPTER XIV.

THE four days which I passed at Choloni were the most miserable I ever experienced in my life, excepting seven which I afterwards spent in Redoute Kaleh. Thanks to the kindness of Mr Longworth, I was as well provided for as was possible under the circumstances, but nothing could make such an existence tolerable. There was no inducement to go outside the tent, for you then found yourself in a pouring rain, standing up to your knees in water. It was equally wretched inside, to sit upon a rickety stool in wet clothes, with one's feet in a puddle, shivering and gazing at vacancy—for our stock of books was exhausted, and we had not even a fire to comfort us, or to change the current of one's thoughts from the contemplation of our own miseries to that of burning embers. Under these circumstances, I generally remained in bed the greater part of the day; and, by tucking a waterproof sheet tightly round my damp blankets, kept in the steam, and under this sort of hydropathic treatment attained artificial warmth.

Fortunately I was too ill to eat anything, as, with the exception of a little rice and biscuit, there was nothing to eat.

At last, upon the morning of the 16th of December, Mr Longworth and I determined to leave the camp, and to try and effect our escape altogether by Redoute Kaleh. Bidding adieu to the few of our countrymen still left with the army, we turned our faces to the storm, and commenced a painful and laborious journey. The first object that met our view was not encouraging : it was that of a man who, just picked out of a ditch, where he had almost perished from cold and starvation, was being laid upon a horse to be carried to camp; but, alas! it was too late. His glassy eyes were fixed in their hollow sockets, and except from a slight convulsive twitching of the fingers, it would have been impossible to know that life was not extinct. It was quite evident that his restoration was beyond all human skill. We ploughed our way wearily along, past waggons hopelessly imbedded in mud, where the bullocks lay down to die, and the Bulgarian drivers, whose pinched and shrunken frames made one wonder how they had ever got so far, seemed about to follow their example—past quantities of dead or gasping horses, and now and then a file of dispirited-looking soldiers, wading and floundering in the mire, following or leading more baggage-animals, who saw their own inevitable destiny in their comrades, with which their path was strewn.

We had been so long wishing to get to Chorga without arriving there, that I began to think that place was a myth. At last the sight of a small collection of Mingrelian huts on one side of the road, and of Turkish tents on the other, cheered our drooping spirits, and we at once made interest with the officer commanding to procure us a hut. There was great difficulty in finding an unoccupied one, as the country-people had been bold enough to remain. Fortunately, however, we discovered a pigsty, with a roof which only leaked in one corner. So, turning the grunting occupants out into the rain, we swept, and, as far as possible, cleansed it, and were soon reconciled to any disagreeable peculiarity in the odour which pervaded it, by the satisfaction of being able to sit by a good wood-fire, a comfort we had not known for weeks.   My trusty Circassian, as usual, devoted himself to making me comfortable ; and after having satisfied his conscience in this respect, informed me that he was very ill, and going to die, but that I need not mind it, as it was of no consequence.   I immediately gave him a dose of camphor and chloroform, a preparation from which I had myself derived great benefit, and with which I ultimately had the satisfaction of curing him.

It was only twelve miles from Chorga to Redoute Kaleh, but the road thither had, during the last few days, become impassable for baggage-animals.   Fortunately water communication, by means of the river Chopi, enabled the army to draw its supplies.   The alternative was presented to us of floundering on horseback, without further loss of time, to Redoute Kaleh, or of waiting for one of the return empty commissariat boats.   We chose the former.   The road lay between the river Chopi and a densely-wooded morass ; in some places these approached so closely to one another that earthen works had been thrown across the narrow neck of land, which would have presented a succession of most formidable obstacles to the advance of an invading army, as it would have been impossible to turn them.

The difficulty of the road, when we traversed it, was enhanced by the inclemency of the weather. The rain had been converted into driving sleet and hail ; and the combined effects of illness, cold, wet, fatigue, and starvation, had almost exhausted me, when, after having been repeatedly bogged and baffled by sloughs and quagmires, I at last, with inexpressible satisfaction, saw the roofs of the houses of Redoute Kaleh. Crossing a stream which here falls into the Chopi, by a rickety bridge, guarded by a no less rickety-looking sentry, we crawled into the fort and looked about us for shelter. All the houses were occupied either as stores or officers' quarters. At last, after some trouble, we obtained possession of a room with a wooden floor, and which was dismally lighted by a small aperture, attached to which swung an apology for a shutter. It was approached by a very dirty

N

passage inhabited by goats, whose presence, however, cheered rather than annoyed us, as they furnished living testimony to the comparative facility with which our larder could be replenished.

Here, too, we could make a fire, and, spreading our blankets on the floor before it, enjoy its genial blaze. Only those who have been deprived for any length of time of the luxury of a fire in the middle of December can really appreciate its consolatory effects, and can understand how the greatest pleasure in life consists in gazing into it with feelings of gratitude, and discover in a constant rearrangement of the logs a most engrossing and delightful occupation. Here tobacco was procurable; and when a man has a pipe to smoke and a fire to look at, what can he desire further to render him supremely happy and contented? Such, at least, was the first conclusion which my enjoyment of these luxuries led me to form. When, however, under their soothing influence, our ideas began to arrange themselves, we remembered that the object of our coming to Redoute Kaleh at all was to escape from it with the least possible delay; and thus, to our dismay, we discovered that, owing to the prevalence of strong westerly winds, the steamers which had been anchored here had been compelled to weigh and stand out to sea, or seek shelter in Batoum. The fact that this proceeding is constantly rendered necessary, forms an insuperable objection to Redoute Kaleh as a point at which to land an army.

For a week we listened in gloomy despondency to the howling storm, and having, during that period, been engaged in the manner I have above described, our notions respecting the summit of human happiness began to change, and we felt that something more was necessary to the enjoyment of existence than tobacco and wood fires. Meantime Omer Pasha and his staff had arrived, in order to make arrangements for the commissariat of the army ; and Colonel Simmons, Colonel Caddell, and Captain M'Intyre appeared bent, like ourselves, upon quitting the dismal scene. I afterwards heard that Colonel Hinde very soon followed their example, leaving Colonel Ballard the only English officer still attached to the army.

During our stay at Redoute Kaleh we were

not altogether devoid of excitement.   Stirring
intelligence arrived one day from the interior,
from which it appeared that the enemy had
not been idle.   Finding that it was useless any
longer to attempt to harass the main body of
the army, Prince Gregoire, at the head of about
five hundred Georgian and Imeritian militia,
had surrounded Sugdidi; and, forcing the unfortunate inhabitants of the neighbouring villages to take up arms, under threat of burning
down their houses in case of refusal, he led an
armed mob into the town in the middle of the
night, and surprised an unfortunate garrison of
a hundred and eighty Turkish soldiers who
had been left there invalided.   Three or four
of these were killed, and thirty-two taken prisoners in their beds, before the alarm had
thoroughly aroused the remainder.   These assembled hastily in the square before the Princess's palace, and not only offered a stout
resistance, but charged their numerous enemy,
who crowded the narrow streets, with such determination that they killed sixty of them,
among whom were eight Beys, and utterly
routed the whole force ; after which they bar-
ricaded themselves in the palace, from which

place a messenger was despatched to Omer Pasha asking for relief, at the same time assuring him they were provisioned and prepared for a long resistance.

Gregoire, finding it was hopeless to attempt to dislodge these brave men, turned his arms against a Mingrelian Bey who had taken up arms with the Turks, and obliged him to fortify himself with his retainers in his romantic fortress, which crowns a hill-top, in regular feudal style. He, too, had applied for assistance, and Skender Pasha was sent to the relief of both parties. That enterprising general, getting information of the presence of the enemy within a few miles of the camp, went out to meet them with a regiment of cavalry and a battalion of Rifles under Colonel Ballard. Placing the Rifles in ambush, he advanced with his cavalry upon Prince Gregoire. Seeing the small force which was opposed to him, the Prince charged the cavalry, which retreated until the enemy was fairly in the trap, when the order was given to fire, and a storm of Minié bullets emptied a hundred saddles on the spot : the remainder precipitately took to their heels. Skender Pasha then proceeded to Sugdidi. Since this

skirmish I have not heard of any hostile movements having been made on either side, and
with it, therefore, all active military operations
for the year, in these provinces, may be said
to have closed.

CHAPTER XV.

THE Transcaucasian campaign of the Turkish army under Omer Pasha having thus terminated, it may not be uninteresting to cast a cursory glance at its results, as affecting not only the interests of the Allies, but of the inhabitants of these provinces themselves. With regard to the first, it seems only lately to have dawned upon the public of England, and not at all upon that of France, that Turkey, whom we were engaged in protecting, had any interest in this quarter of the globe. This probably arose from the circumstance that, until the siege of Kars induced them to open their maps, they were ignorant of the fact that Russia had any territory in this direction. Upon no other hypothesis is it possible to comprehend why some measures were not taken at an earlier period of the war to injure

Russia where she is most vulnerable, and to protect Turkey where she is most exposed. Had it not been that Kars was besieged, it is pretty certain that this campaign, which was, whether rightly or wrongly, designed to relieve it, would never have been attempted. Had it been undertaken at a sufficiently early period of the year, and with such troops as would have insured success, military and political results would have been attained, among which the salvation of Kars would have been the most certain, but at the same time the least important. Even now the value of an aggressive movement is being depreciated in favour of defensive operations upon the Turkish frontier, and we are infinitely more inclined to devote our energies to defending Erzeroum than to attacking Tiflis ; and yet, by adopting this latter course, we not only cut off the Russian army and save Erzeroum as effectually as if we sent 100,000 men there, but we deprive Russia of territory more than three times as great in extent as the United Kingdom of Great Britain and Ireland. It is not necessary, however, to recapitulate here all the advantages which would result from this movement. I have already endeavoured to point them out in a pamphlet* which I published a year ago, urging the propriety of this very campaign, and predicting the disastrous events which have since taken place in Anatolia. While peaceful negotiations are pending, however, all speculations upon future military operations are to a certain extent deprived of their interest. At the same time, we may be permitted to hope that, in the event of these negotiations being broken off, and hostilities being again resumed, the attention of our ally may be a little more specially directed to this quarter of the world, in which she has just as important interests at stake as ourselves, inasmuch as the gradual absorption of Asia Minor, and extension of the Russian frontier to the Asiatic shores of the Bosphorus, would affect the balance of power in Europe far more than the tranquillity of India.

Should, indeed, the Allied Powers be compelled to recommence hostilities, and determine upon operating in these provinces, it will be found that the campaign of Omer Pasha has

---

* *The Transcaucasian Provinces the proper Field of Operation for a Christian Army.*

not been utterly unproductive of good results ; whilst if it had been undertaken one week earlier, and he had reached Kutais, it would have been invested with great importance, not merely in a military point of view, but as introducing a new political feature into the present peace negotiations.

Had the Turkish army gone into winter-quarters at Kutais, Omer Pasha would have received there the adhesion of the Princess Dadianie, as well as that of the principal families of Imeritia and Gouriel. Prince Michael had already given in his submission. At this moment Russia would have found herself deprived of four provinces (two of which are amongst the most valuable of her possessions beyond the Caucasus), containing altogether a population of about 500,000 souls, and an area of double that of the Crimea. She would have had no reason to congratulate herself upon her recent siege on these terms, and the possession of the capital of Imeritia might fairly have been deemed more than equivalent in political value to the conquest of Kars. There can be no doubt that, under these circumstances, should peace be made, a very different arrangement would be effected with reference to the Asiatic dominions of Russia, from that which will be the result of the Paris negotiations. If peace be not made, we should be in a far more favourable attitude to recommence the war. During the whole of this winter, Omer Pasha would have been occupied in establishing depôts at Kutais, with a view to making it the base of operations for the spring. The resources of the surrounding provinces would have poured into the town, and the population, if not absolutely friendly, would have been awed into good behaviour.

It would have been quite impossible for Mouravieff to have advanced upon Kutais until the spring. The only quarter from which an attack was to be feared was Akhaltsik, and that could have been watched. The Rhion, navigable to Mehranie, only three hours from Kutais, would have formed the line of communication by which ammunition, reinforcements, and the material of war could have been transported during the winter ; and, if necessary, an Allied army concentrated preparatory to an advance upon Tiflis. The advantages which would have been gained by possessing a starting-point, eighty miles from the sea-board, in an enemy's country, amid a friendly population, and with a safe and convenient line of water-communication, will be readily admitted.

It is melancholy to think that we should have only been prevented from obtaining this great political and military position, by the timidity or obstinacy of those who, by detaining the Turkish army in the Crimea until the beginning of October, delayed operations until so late a period of the year, that the campaign, the history of which I have endeavoured to relate, should have proved abortive.

That any results should have sprung from it at all, only shows how much greater they might have been. What these are may briefly be described : In the event of war, the march from Souchoum Kaleh, and the battle of the Ingour, have secured the left flank of the Turkish army ; the friendly co-operation of one province, Abkhasia, has been obtained : the prestige of Russia in Mingrelia has been destroyed ; the capital of the province is in our hands ; some of its principal chiefs have compromised themselves ; and the population generally, so far as it was possible to judge, have shown themselves well disposed to assist a

Christian army. The position of Choloni, where, to the best of my belief, the Turkish army still remains, is valuable in a strategical point of view, as an advance from it would serve as a formidable diversion in favour of an army operating in any other quarter; while it offers a most convenient starting-point for a more important movement, and one which, had the Russians been a little more prepared, could not have been gained without great risk and loss of life. The most difficult part of any campaign in this direction, consists in the disembarkation of the army on a coast almost devoid of harbours, and the first advance through an enemy's country intersected by rivers and swamps, and at some seasons of the year very unhealthy. To have landed an army at Redoute Kaleh, and forced the difficult and defensible road to Choloni, would have been quite impracticable. But now depôts of provisions may be formed there and at Sugdidi; and an army landed at Souchoum would reach the latter place in five days, and in five more arrive at Kutais.

In the event of peace, it is to be hoped that the policy which Prince Michael found himself compelled by the presence of a Turkish army to adopt, may induce us to make some stipulations in his favour ; and that Abkhasia, now once more freed from the Russian yoke, may be rendered thoroughly independent. This concession will not be without its political significance in the eyes of the neighbouring Circassians ; indeed, it will have a tendency to weaken Russian influence in the East generally, and therefore be of importance to the Allies.   But it is also due to the Prince, who, if deserted by us, and allowed again to subside into a condition of Russian servitude, would doubtless receive from that amiable power a full compensation for what she terms the treachery of his conduct in not following the example of his prudent sister-in-law, and retiring into the mountains.

That the position of the Mingrelians is no less unfortunate, was exemplified by the affair at Sugdidi.   Forced, on the one hand, by the brother of their sovereign to take up arms against the Turks ; subject, on the other, to the immediate vengeance of these, the present possessors of the country, if they are caught with arms, they have been placed in a dilemma from which they see no escape, as it

involves the destruction of all they hold dear
to them.

If the conduct of the Princess has not been
such as to warrant our demanding her independence, the predicament in which her subjects find themselves at present placed, as well
as their behaviour in not opposing our progress, entitles them to some consideration,
whilst the position we hold in the country
gives us a right to make certain demands. It
would be doubly desirable if these could be of
such a nature as to enable us, whilst watching
over our own interests, to promote those of the
Mingrelians.

Both these objects, as it appears to me,
might be gained by stipulations which should
have the effect of abolishing those mercantile
restrictions which have retarded the progress
of the province, and of doing away with that
monopoly of trade which Russia purchased at
Redoute Kaleh alone, but which she most un-
justly exercises throughout the whole length
of the coast. By throwing Mingrelia open to
commercial enterprise, a new and profitable
market would be created for our manufactures,
whilst the resources of the country would be

developed, and the prosperity of the population proportionately advanced. It does not seem that in making these demands we should be asking, either with respect to Abkhasia or Mingrelia, more than we have a right to expect ; but whether we make peace and obtain independence for one, and free trade for the other ; or make war, and gain only a valuable strategical position for ourselves, let us hope that those political and military men who have hitherto riveted their delighted gaze upon the shattered docks of Sebastopol, may extend the range of their mental vision to the opposite shore of the Black Sea ; and as they gradually acquire a hazy consciousness of the existence of Russia in that quarter, may admit that the campaign which has just been prosecuted in those newly-discovered regions has not been altogether barren of political and military results.

APPENDIX.

THE following pages, in which the expediency of a campaign in the Transcaucasian provinces is advocated, were written about six months ago, when no such undertaking, so far as I was aware, was in contemplation.

At that time public interest was concentrated in the Crimea, and any scheme of operations in a more remote quarter of the Russian dominions was regarded with a somewhat unfavourable eye, probably because the political considerations which attached to these provinces were as little understood by the world in general as their geographical position. Now, however, that the campaign of Omer Pasha has attracted universal attention to the acquisitions of Russia beyond the Caucasus, I venture again to submit to the public my former observations upon them.

As I do not happen to have a copy of my pamphlet with me, and as, during my journey with the Turkish army through some of these provinces, opportunities have been afforded to me of acquiring more ample information upon the subject, I shall avail myself of this occasion to notice, as briefly as possible, one or two additional considerations, in which the interests of the Allied Powers are more immediately concerned.

o

With the exception of Abkhasia, in which the population is partly Mahommedan and partly Christian, and some
of the more southern Armenian provinces, the people of
Transcaucasia are for the most part Christians.   It is
therefore natural that they should look with extreme dis-
trust upon the progress of a Mussulman army through their
country, since they regard a successful campaign by a
Turkish general as the inevitable prelude to annexation to
the dominions of the Sultan ; and that they should moreover hesitate, before transferring their allegiance from the
Czar to the Padisha, to consider how far their political
condition would be ameliorated by such a change.   Under
these circumstances, the alternative which they have chosen
is by no means remarkable ; nor can we wonder at the
suspicious attitude which they have assumed upon the
arrival upon their frontier of the army deputed by the
Allied Powers to free them from a bondage which, though
detestable in their eyes, seemed less to be dreaded than
that into which they believe themselves about to fall.
Although the operations of Omer Pasha's army hitherto
have been most fortunate, it is very doubtful whether, if
the populations of these provinces remain in determined
hostility to him, he will be enabled to prosecute a campaign with success next year, as he becomes farther removed from his base of operations.   It is therefore desirable to consider whether (the object for which the expedition to the Crimea having been to a certain extent gained)
a portion of the army should not in spring be withdrawn
from that peninsula, and thrown into these provinces.   The
appearance of a Christian army will not only enlist the
sympathies of the Christian population, but, whether that
army be English, French, or Sardinian, the possibility of
ultimate annexation to any of these Powers will be too
remote to create any apprehension.

In the event of such an undertaking, two questions naturally arise,—first, What is to become of the Turkish army when a Christian army comes here? and, secondly, What is to become of the Transcaucasian provinces when it goes away?

The first of these questions is easily answered. The real field of operations for a Turkish force is that part of the country which lies between the Kuban and the Caucasian range. Here the population inhabiting the Caucasian provinces of Natquoitch, Bsaduch, Hattoquoi, Demigoi, Beslinoi, and the two Kabardas, are Mahommedan to a man; they have an engrained and profound veneration for the person of the Sultan; they are thoroughly anti-Russian, for they have carried on a war with successive Czars, with varied success, for upwards of half a century; and they desire nothing more earnestly than an opportunity of rallying round the standard of a Turkish general in a war with the Giaours. Their country is as fertile as its inhabitants are brave. Stretching away upon the northern slopes of the Caucasus in a series of beautiful undulating plains, it is capable of sustaining a large army. A glance at the map will show the result of such a movement in a strategical point of view; and the facility with which all communication through the Pass of Dariel could be intercepted would extremely harass a Russian army, if it were at the same time engaged with a formidable enemy upon the other side. The Turkish army could be transferred without difficulty from Souchoum Kaleh to Sudjak Kaleh, whence a military road leads into the plains of the Kuban, a distance of only twenty miles, and which would thenceforward become the base of operations.

With regard to the second question, viz., the ultimate destiny of the Transcaucasian provinces, it does not seem very difficult of solution. They desire nothing more earnestly than to be left alone; and certainly we could pursue no course which would be attended with less difficulty than that of meeting their wishes in this respect. If a Christian army encamping in this country guaranteed each province it passed through its independence, there can be no doubt that the population would be ready and willing to offer every assistance. To such a policy two objections are usually started. One is, that by offering such a guarantee we commit ourselves ever afterwards to protect the province; and the other is, that having, when we engaged in this war, laid it down as a principle that we would not deprive Russia of territory, we are not now entitled to depart from it. With regard to the first objection, the consideration which arises is, on what side is aggression on these provinces to be feared? If from Turkey (and it is doubtful whether she will ever again be in a condition to aggress), we can always make our own will respected without going to war with her. If from Russia, it is one of the objects of this pamphlet to show that it is our interest always to prevent Russia from acquiring territory to the south of the Caucasus, even if it involves a war. Most certain it is, at all events, that we cannot expect these populations to rise to our assistance, unless we offer to protect them from the retributive vengeance of that Power, whose displeasure they will have incurred by taking up arms against her. With regard to the other objection, it is scarcely worth noticing. It certainly was a remarkable thing that, when we engaged in a war to protect the integrity and independence of the Ottoman Empire, we should have volunteered the same kind offices in behalf of the Power whose aggressive tendencies we were fighting to repress. But even if we consider ourselves still bound by this principle,—and the English public is beginning strongly to object to it,—we shall be relieved of responsibility on this score, for Russia will never make a peace honourable to England, unless she is driven to it ; and she will never be driven to it, unless we deprive her of territory. As the speediest mode, therefore, of bringing about this most desirable result, preparations should immediately be made for sending a Christian army into the Transcaucasian provinces early next year, which should co-operate with the Turkish army upon the plains of the Kuban.

TURKISH CAMP, SUGDIDI, MINGRELIA,
13th *November*.

The following is an extract from the pamphlet in which, after having considered the difficulties attendant upon a Crimean campaign, and its merits in a political point of view, I have endeavoured to show the greater feasibility of one in the Transcaucasian provinces, and the superior importance of its political results :—

The extent of any evacuation of the Crimea must depend upon local considerations, and it will be for those on the spot to decide upon the practicability of retaining the whole peninsula of Chersonese, as comprised within the lines of the old Heraclean wall, which extends from Balaklava to Inkermann,—and thence by the present line of Russian defences to the north of Sebastopol ; or if that be too great an undertaking, to consider the relative merits of Balaklava, Sebastopol, or Eupatoria separately, as permanent garrisons. In any case we should be obliged to leave a large force behind ; and it would be a strong recommendation to the proposed plan of operation elsewhere, that a comparatively small army would be required for its execution.

It will hardly be questioned that, had we originally landed in the Transcaucasian provinces, a much smaller army than that which has for seven months been cooped up in a corner of the Crimea would have sufficed to drive the Russians beyond those mountain ranges which form the natural boundary of the empire in this direction.

A total misconception seems to prevail with regard to the physical character of the eastern shores of the Black Sea ; and the project of an expedition to Mingrelia and Imeritia has been stamped as visionary, on account of the " mountainous and impracticable nature of the country near the coast." It is to be hoped that correct information may induce a change of opinion upon this point, and that means may be taken to obtain it.

It will be found that Mingrelia, the southern part of Imeritia, and the northern portion of Gouriel, from Anaklea to Shefkatil, comprising a tract about eighty miles in length by sixty in breadth, is a perfectly level plain covered with forest, and intersected by the Rhion and its innumerable tributaries. A great part of this flat land is marshy, and consequently in some seasons of the year unhealthy ; while, if it were proposed to campaign in this province, a more valid objection to such a proceeding would be found in the denseness of its forests than in the height of its mountains.

Redoute Kaleh, the most important Russian port upon the coast, and Poti, at the mouth of the Rhion, might be held as the base of operation. The Rhion itself, a remarkably deep stream, with upwards of seven feet of water on the bar, would enable us to convey our troops in steamers of light draught for sixty miles to Mehranie, and form an admirable line of communication, which could be protected, if necessary, by the inhabitants of the country, whose feelings of hostility to the Russians would prompt them willingly to lend their aid. A range, crossed by roads constructed by Russian engineers, divides the low country from the high table-land of Georgia, and here our progress would probably, in the first instance, be opposed.

It would be impossible, however, for the Russians to concentrate any very large force at one point, for they are compelled to scatter their army, estimated at about fifty thousand men, over the country, in order to repress any outbreak on the part of the native population, who are only watching for an opportunity to give effectual assistance to the enemies of their hated oppressors. This inconvenience was seriously felt by them during last year's campaign against the Turks. The Allied forces, if provided with a good commissariat, and ample means of land-transport, which a campaign in the Crimea must equally involve, would have the additional advantage here, of a population more willing and able to contribute supplies, and of a country far more fertile in its resources, possessing a climate both milder in winter and healthier in summer.

If anything further need be said in support of the feasibility of such an enterprise, it is worthy of remark that in 1828 a Russian army of eighteen thousand, opposed to a Turkish army of thirty thousand men, invaded these provinces ; and in the course of one campaign the towns of Poti, Anapa, Diadeen, Bayazid, Toprakalè, and Ardahan fell into the hands of the Czar. Surely, when a Russian army can successfully overrun a disaffected country, occupied by a hostile force, an Anglo-French army would, with the assistance of a friendly population, have no ground for discouragement. With the co-operation on the north of the redoubtable Schamyl, and his invincible Lesghis, who have for more than a quarter of a century defied the whole military force of Russia—supported on the south by Turkish troops—welcomed by a native population burning to resent the wrongs they have suffered as a conquered people—with our own ships to fall back upon—a richly cultivated, well-watered country to operate in, and a Russian army to oppose comparatively insignificant in extent, and which could only be reinforced with the utmost difficulty from Astrakhan across the Caspian,—the allied forces of England and France might last year have invaded the country under circumstances which could not have failed to insure success.

But it is not with the view of reflecting upon those councils which dictated the expedition to the Crimea that these remarks are made, for, with our previous knowledge of the defenceless state of Sebastopol, the unfortunate results of that enterprise could never have been anticipated ; but rather to call attention to the fact that, whatever, at the commencement of the war, may have been the difference of opinions as to the relative merits of an expedition to the Crimea and one to the Transcaucasian provinces, those arguments which were advanced in favour of the latter now far outweigh any which can be brought to support the expediency of a campaign in a rocky peninsula, after the object with which it was originally invaded has been achieved. And it will be easy to prove that, even if we were to admit that the difficulties attendant upon a campaign in the one country were as many and as great as we have shown them to be in the other, the political advantages which we should gain by the expulsion of the Russians from the countries beyond the Caucasus, would be of much higher importance than those which would result from a similar success in the Crimea ; while the geographical position of the former would render them more easy to retain. With our cruisers upon the west coast, it would be impossible for Russia to throw in troops by way of the Black Sea ; to the Circassians, who know so well how to protect their native hills, might safely be left the defence of the passes of Mozdok and Derbent, the only practicable entrances by land for Russian troops into Georgia ;—the extent of the Russian fleet upon the Caspian is totally inadequate to the transport of any force from Astrakhan, sufficiently powerful to land in the face of a hostile army, which might be composed principally of Turks, supported by a few thousands of the Allied troops. On the other hand, we dare not attempt to estimate the strength of the Allied army which it would be necessary to encamp upon the arid plains of the Northern Crimea, and to the destruction of which would be devoted the whole military energies and resources of Russia.

If it be granted then, in the first place, that a campaign in the Transcaucasian provinces would be as practicable, in a military point of view, as one in the Crimea ; and in the second, that the retention of the former would be a much more easy task, and require a far smaller force than the occupation of the latter, it only remains for us to consider the superior political advantages which would result from the successful prosecution of the war upon the Asiatic frontier of the empire. It may safely be asserted that the balance of power in Europe depends in some measure upon the balance of power in Asia. " The integrity and independence of the Ottoman Empire" has certainly been threatened upon the banks of the Araxes as often as upon the shores of the Danube, and Muscovite Czars have exercised as much skill both in war and diplomacy to make

the Caspian a Russian lake as to extend their dominions
beyond the Black Sea ; whilst their designs, not having
been so narrowly watched, have been crowned with much
greater success.   They have thus been enabled to acquire
territory from Turkey in Asia equal in extent to the whole
of the smaller states of Germany,—from Persia, equal in
extent to England,—and to advance their frontier a thousand miles in a south-easterly direction.   The Kirghiz and
Turcoman tribes inhabiting the steppes upon the east of
the Caspian, are completely under the influence of Russia
as far south as the Attruck, which forms the northern
boundary of Persia.   The only shore of the Caspian, therefore, which is not Russian, is the southern, about four hundred miles in length, and composed of the long-coveted
and fertile Persian provinces of Ghilan, Mazenderan, and
Astrabad, the two former of which, Mr Curzon tells us, are
already mortgaged to Russia for a debt of £2,000,000.
By the treaty of Goolistan, Russia reserves to herself the
exclusive right of navigating the Caspian with ships of
war.

From the most eastern point of the Black Sea to the
most eastern point of the Caspian, the naval and military
forces of Russia menace the frontiers of Turkey and of
Persia ; we already know what the effect has been of her
arms upon the one country, we have yet to learn the results of her diplomacy in the other, and to hope that the
influence which has heretofore been so powerfully exercised
by Russia in the prosecution of her ambitious designs, may
not again prevail in the councils of the Shah ; and in the
expression of this hope we would disclaim the imputation
of any interested motives, or that the proposal to carry on
the war at a more eastern point arises out of selfish considerations connected with our Indian empire.   The following opinion, expressed many years ago by one who was

formerly the British minister in Persia, will be an answer to any such insinuations : " The acquisition by Russia of a control over the power and resources of Turkey and Persia (*and the one implies the other*), would be dangerous to the existence of Austria, to the commerce and Indian possessions of England ; it would endanger the tranquillity of the southern states of Europe, *especially of France*, and give to Russia a preponderance, which would put in imminent peril the independence of more than one nation, the liberties of more than one people." If, therefore, all Europe is, as it has professed itself to be, interested in the preservation of Turkey ; and if, as will be shown, the most formidable attack upon it which could be made from any quarter is from Persia, any proposal which, together with other advantages, would include that of rendering such an attack almost impossible, is worthy of being entertained by the Allied Powers.

In the event of Persia declaring in favour of Russia while the Allied armies are engaged in operating in the Crimea, the position of matters in Asiatic Turkey will be rendered desperate. The entire military resources of the Eastern portion of the Ottoman dominions are concentrated in Armenia, in defence of a frontier line nearly three hundred miles in extent, extending from Fort St Nicholai (or Shefkatil), on the Black Sea, to the point on the Araxes at which the Persian frontier meets those of Russia and Turkey. The experience of last summer has proved it incompetent for this task. In the mean time, there remains an undefended frontier of more than seven hundred miles in length, extending from Bayazid to Bussora. Never before has such an opportunity been presented to Persia of acquiring the long-coveted Pashalik of Bagdad. It is not very difficult to predict the result of an invasion of this remote and exposed province, by a

fanatical army, whose feelings are roused into greater activity by religious enthusiasm.   Meanwhile, the Turkish
troops, already overmatched by the forces of the Czar,
will be taken directly in flank by the victorious Persians,
and the provinces of Kars and Erzeroum will be at the
mercy of the combined armies.   It is scarcely necessary
to speculate further upon the consequences of such an
event, or upon the moral effect which it would exercise
upon every people in Asia.   But if, on the other hand,
Russia were deprived of her Transcaucasian provinces,
her influence in Persia is utterly destroyed.   The defence
of the southern frontier of Armenia may be left to the inhabitants themselves, well qualified to resist Persian aggression ; while the Turkish army, relieved of the presence
of their most dreaded enemy, might meet the new invaders
upon equal terms.   Upon the East, the Affghans, true to
their spiritual allegiance to the Sultan, would pour down
like a flood upon the presumptuous schismatics, and the
presence of a few thousand troops at Karak, or Bushire,
would render the issue of the war no longer doubtful.

Ever since the commencement of the war, Persia, bound
to Russia by pecuniary obligations, and fanatically opposed
to Turkey on religious grounds, but at the same time
dreading to incur the displeasure of the Western Powers by
allying herself to Russia, has remained undecided in her
policy ; but it may confidently be asserted, that upon the
landing of an Anglo-French army in the Transcaucasian
provinces, she would at once declare for the Western
Powers.   One advantage then arising out of such an expedition, would be the conversion of a power capable of being
one of our most formidable enemies, into a most valuable
ally, whose active co-operation would be equivalent to a
guarantee for the safety of Asiatic Turkey.

But while the common object with which the war was

originally undertaken—viz., the protection of the Sultan's dominions—may be thus in a great measure achieved, the humiliation of Russia is also one in which the Western Powers are no less united ; and this would certainly be involved by that territorial deprivation which would be the result of success in the expedition now proposed. In the present state of our political relations upon the continent of Europe, there is no portion of the Russian dominions there of which she could be permanently shorn. Finland is out of the question, because we have alienated the Fins, by blockading their coasts and burning their villages. Poland is not to be calculated upon, because we have placed ourselves in antagonism to the revolutionary element of Europe, by attempting to conciliate its despots. Bessarabia must ever remain an oppressed province of Russia, for its population is deficient in vitality. The Crimea might be temporarily occupied, but to hope permanently to annex to Turkey this distant peninsula, which is now an integral portion of the Russian empire, would be as absurd as to imagine that it could be organised into an independent kingdom. But none of these objections exist in the case of the provinces beyond the Caucasus. We have not, as in Finland, given their inhabitants cause for complaint, beyond manifesting an extreme want of interest in their concerns. Nor have they, like the Poles, lost confidence in us, for we have not been engaged for two years in unsuccessful attempts to propitiate powers upon their frontiers, whose interests are directly opposed to theirs. Their vital energies have not been crushed by a long course of Muscovite oppression, or their hopes of freedom almost extinguished, as in the less favoured province of Bessarabia. While comprising territory four times in extent that of the Tauric peninsula, containing a population proportionately exceeding it in amount, and formed, not of

dejected Tartars, but of the most hardy and enterprising
race in the world, with a frontier conterminous with that
of Turkey for 300 miles—these provinces are in a totally
different position from the Crimea, and are capable either
of independent organisation, or of such arrangement with
respect to Turkey, at the end of the war, as may be deemed
consistent with the interests of that empire, and serve at
the same time as a more effectual barrier to Russian
aggression in the East—an advantage which would not be
involved by the severance of the Crimea from the dominions of the Czar, even were such a project feasible, since
that province is completely isolated, and touches the
frontier of no other country.

A consideration of these circumstances, then, fairly war-
rants the assertion, that the Allied Powers are severally and
collectively interested in the success of a campaign in the
Transcaucasian provinces, since it is here alone that any
definite and decisive results can be hoped for.   But it
would not be fair to our allies to say that we are all *equally*
interested.   Doubtless this country has interests at stake
in the East, which will be deeply affected for good or evil
by the results of the war in this direction.   Whatever may
have been the popular opinion some years back, when the
public were almost entirely uninformed upon Asiatic
politics, there are comparatively few now so ignorant of
them as to maintain that it is a matter of indifference to
England whether Russian influence, or, in other words, the
Russian frontier, is extended to Herat,—and our Indian
possessions are only separated by one hostile State from
that empire.   Without, therefore, entering more fully into
a discussion of this point, we may regard it as an established fact, that Russia has for many years past been carrying on intrigues in the independent states of Central
Asia and has sought to coerce Persia, not only through

Armenia, but through Khiva—hence those rumours which have so often reached this country of a Russian army at Khiva. But if we carry out the undertaking now proposed, we shall have no more such rumours. A Russian army in Khiva, even if it could ever get there, unsupported by one in Armenia, would find itself in a particularly useless position; and even in connection with the Affghans and Turcomans, could hope to gain no advantage over a power which, now that the tide of Russian aggression had been stayed, no longer believed in Russian omnipotence, as it saw with amazement that the Allied Powers of Europe had been able to maintain the tottering independence of plundered and enfeebled Turkey.

A consideration of the present state of the acquired provinces in Asia will bring us to the conclusion, that the extension of the frontier line of Russia to the east of the Caspian must be regulated entirely by its progress to the west of that sea, and that it is in the power of this country to check that progress at once, and thus nip in the bud her long-cherished designs upon Persia, and her deeply-laid schemes for the appropriation of those sources of wealth and power in the East, which have so materially contributed to raise this country to her present high position among European nations.* Not only would our Indian Empire be thus secured from the risk of civil commotion arising from insidious foreign interference, but the extensive and valuable trade which is now being carried on between England and Persia, by way of Trebizond, would be put beyond the chance of that interruption which, in the case of a Russian advance to Erzeroum, is inevitable, and may not improbably lead to its ultimate annihilation.

* This subject has been more fully discussed by the writer in an article entitled "The Progress and Policy of Russia in Central Asia," *Blackwood's Magazine*, May 1854. Also, see *The Russian Shores of the Black Sea*, page 221.

It therefore does not seem too much to expect that an enterprise which affects the interests of all the Allied powers to a great extent, and of one of them most deeply, should be undertaken without delay ; for it is probable that such an opportunity of attacking Russia at a remote and most vulnerable point may never again occur, as presents itself at this juncture, when a well-equipped army of one hundred and fifty thousand men is distant from it only two days' sail.   And if our allies do not perceive the full importance of such a step, in so far as their interests are concerned, we at least can have no such doubt ; and it may well be urged in favour of a descent by the English army *alone* upon those provinces, that the cordiality at present subsisting between England and France would in no way be impaired by their armies being engaged in different fields of operation, but that, on the contrary, each would more effectively develop its characteristic mode of warfare, when unhampered by the presence of the other ; and that divided command which even now destroys the vigour of our siege operations, and which cannot possibly continue throughout a summer campaign, would at once cease.

With a combined naval and military attack in the Baltic, a French army in the Crimea, and an English army in the Caucasus—to oppose which it would be impossible to send reinforcements—the Czar would be seriously embarrassed.   If, on the other hand, some such step is not taken, and that speedily, the experience of last year leads us to predict that the Turkish army at Erzeroum will again be beaten,* and the Russians possibly occupy that city ; and if so, this time they will not quit it.   The effect of the advance of Russia in 1829 was felt

* This anticipation has been already justified with respect to Kars.

all through the East.   It will be tenfold greater when it is made in defiance of the united armies of England and France.

In conclusion, it would be well that those who propose a campaign in the Crimea alone, should be prepared for the consequences of such a proceeding ; and, when the Russian armies have either been driven or have retired beyond the Isthmus of Perecop, know beforehand how to meet that contingency which we are hopeful enough to suppose would be inevitable.   Are we to follow the example of Napoleon, and march to Moscow after them ; or are we to be encamped upon the desolate Isthmus for an indefinite time, exposed to war, famine, and pestilence ; or are we to re-embark and go to the Caucasus when it is too late, and the Russians occupy the mountain-passes of Armenia ; or do we flatter ourselves that the " safe and honourable peace," in search of which our statesmen occasionally make pilgrimages to Vienna, will be found there in consequence of such an event ?   Let us have a distinct notion of what is to come after this campaign in the Crimea, that the country may know what its army is fighting for, and our soldiers be cheered in the hour of victory ; or, in default of any such schemes for the future, let us not regard a campaign in the Transcaucasian provinces as a " wild notion," because we had " no notion " where they were until we looked upon the map.   There, at least, our efforts will be attended with definite results ;——we shall deprive Russia of a portion of her empire equal in extent to Prussia ; we shall render her further aggression upon Persia and Turkey impossible ; we shall utterly, destroy her prestige throughout Asia, save our own transit trade, and be entirely relieved of apprehension with regard to India.   We shall free an oppressed and enslaved people,

P

in all probability capable themselves of guarding their
own frontier, but with whom if it is necessary to leave
a small force, they will be well cared for, in a healthy
climate and fertile country ; and ultimately, by means
of a rigorous and *bonâ fide* blockade of her whole mari-
time provinces, and the adoption of such other measures
as may effectually destroy her commerce, frame a basis
for negotiation very different in its character from that
which has been so scornfully rejected, and of which a
" fifth point " should be, that between the Black Sea and
the Caspian, the Terek and the Kuban do henceforward
form the frontier of Russia.

ATHENÆUM CLUB,
18*th May* 1855.

PRINTED BY WILLIAM BLACKWOOD AND SONS, EDINBURGH.

WORKS PUBLISHED
BY
WILLIAM BLACKWOOD AND SONS,
EDINBURGH AND LONDON.

SIR ARCHIBALD ALISON'S NEW HISTORY.

THE HISTORY OF EUROPE,

FROM THE FALL OF NAPOLEON TO THE ACCESSION OF LOUIS NAPOLEON.

By Sir Archibald Alison, Bart., D.C.L.

Four Volumes are published.
Uniform with the Library Edition of the Author's "History of Europe," price 15s.

THE HISTORY OF EUROPE,

FROM THE COMMENCEMENT OF THE FRENCH REVOLUTION IN 1789 TO THE BATTLE OF WATERLOO.

By Sir Archibald Alison, Bart., D.C.L.

Library Edition (the Eighth), Fourteen Volumes Demy Octavo, with Portraits, £10, 10s.
Crown Octavo Edition, Twenty Volumes, £6.

ATLAS TO ALISON'S HISTORY OF EUROPE.

By A. Keith Johnston, F.R.S.E., &c.

Author of the "Physical Atlas," &c.

109 Maps and Plans of Countries, Battles, Sieges, and Sea-Fights, Coloured. Demy Quarto, to accompany the Library Edition, and other Editions of the History in Octavo, £3, 3s. Crown Quarto, to accompany the Edition in Crown Octavo, £2, 12s. 6d.

EPITOME
OF
ALISON'S HISTORY OF EUROPE,
FOR THE USE OF SCHOOLS AND YOUNG PERSONS.

Ninth Edition, price 7s. 6d. bound.

" A masterly epitome."—*Hull Packet.*
" A capital piece of work, which, though primarily designed for schools and young persons, will be found very useful to all, as a *coup d'œil* of the History of Europe during one of its most important periods."—*Spectator*

PARIS AFTER WATERLOO.

NOTES TAKEN AT THE TIME, AND HITHERTO UNPUBLISHED; INCLUDING A REVISED
EDITION—THE TENTH—OF A

VISIT TO FLANDERS AND THE FIELD.

By James Simpson, Esq., Advocate.

Author of "The Philosophy of Education," "Lectures to the Working Classes," &c.
With Two Coloured Plans of the Battle.   Crown Octavo, price 5s.

"Numerous as are the accounts of Waterloo that have been published, Mr Simpson's
description may still be read with pleasure, from its freshness; it has the life of vegetation
newly gathered—smacking of reality, little of books."—*Spectator.*

---o---

A New Edition, being the Third.

THE LIFE OF MARLBOROUGH.

By Sir Archibald Alison, Bart. D.C.L.

Two Volumes Demy Octavo, with Maps and Portraits, price 30s.

"Unquestionably the best 'Life of Marlborough.'"—*Morning Post.*
"Alison's 'Life of Marlborough' is an enchaining romance."—*Blackwood's Magazine.*

---o---

Fourth Edition, Demy Octavo, price 12s. 6d.

CURRAN AND HIS CONTEMPORARIES.

By Charles Phillips, Esq., B.A.

"Certainly one of the most extraordinary pieces of Biography ever produced. . . . .
No library should be without it."—*Lord Brougham.*

---o---

Three Volumes Octavo, price £1, 16s.

A HISTORY OF MISSIONS.

By the Rev. W. Brown, M.D.

"We know not where else to find, within the same compass, so much well-digested and
reliable information on the subject of Missions as in these volumes. The study of them will
inspire the reader with new views of the importance, responsibility, and dignity of the Mis-
sionary work."—*American Bibliotheca Sacra.*

THE STORY OF THE
CAMPAIGN OF SEBASTOPOL.
WRITTEN IN THE CAMP.

By Lieut.-Col. E. Bruce Hamley,
Captain, R.A.

Originally published in *Blackwood's Magazine*.
With Illustrations, drawn in Camp by the Author, price 21s.

---o---

THE POSITION ON THE ALMA.
A COLOURED PANORAMIC VIEW, DONE ON THE FIELD.

By Lieut.-Col. E. Bruce Hamley,
Captain, R.A.

Price Ten Shillings and Sixpence.

" Along with this you will get some sketches of the Alma done on the spot, and worked up since I got my colour-box, &c., which were on board ship."—*Extract from Lieut.-Col. Hamley's Letter, Camp before Sebastopol, 29th December* 1854.

---o---

Two Volumes, price £1, 7s. 6d.
HISTORY OF THE BYZANTINE AND
GREEK EMPIRES, 716-1453.

By George Finlay, Esq., Athens.

" It is the most complete and elaborate history of the Byzantine and Greek Empires that has appeared in an English form."—*Leader*.

" At a time when so much attention is being devoted to the modern history of the Greek race, and to the constitution and history of the Greek Church, and when even our scholars are catching the enthusiasm, and insisting on the necessity of studying the modern Greek language and literature, Mr Finlay's solid and careful works will be welcomed by all who read to be informed."—*Athenæum*.

" Mr Finlay's work deserves warm praise as a careful and conscientious performance. General readers might desire that their taste for ' interesting' details should have been provided for by the author. But the judicious and the scholarly will admire the severe abstinence that imparts a Doric severity to this manly and most creditable historical performance, which must confer no small distinction on its author's name."—*Press*.

By the same Author.
I. GREECE UNDER THE ROMANS, B.C. 146 TO A.D. 717. Octavo, 16s.
II. MEDIÆVAL GREECE, 1204-1461. Octavo, 12s.

---o---

MISS STRICKLAND'S LIVES OF THE
QUEENS OF SCOTLAND.
EMBELLISHED WITH PORTRAITS AND HISTORICAL VIGNETTES.

Volumes I. to V. are published, price 10s. 6d. each.

" Embracing a period in the annals of Scotland remarkable for the deeds of violence that were perpetrated in it, and presenting a picture of life and morality strongly contrasting with the results of modern civilisation, she has had a noble field within which to exercise her extraordinary talents for research, and has produced an historical narrative, unsurpassed, in point of interest and intrinsic merit, by any of those which have earned for her the high literary reputation she so deservedly enjoys."—*Morning Advertiser*.

THE POEMS OF FELICIA HEMANS.

Complete in One Volume Large Octavo, with Portrait engraved by FINDEN, 21s.

Another Edition in Six Volumes Foolscap Octavo, 24s.

Another Edition, with Life, by her Sister, Seven Volumes, 35s.

" Of no modern writer can it be affirmed, with less hesitation, that she has become an English Classic, nor, until human nature becomes very different from what it now is, can we imagine the least probability that the music of her lays will cease to soothe the ear, or the beauty of her sentiment to charm the gentle heart."—*Blackwood's Magazine.*

---o---

Twenty-second Edition, Foolscap Octavo, price 7s. 6d.

THE COURSE OF TIME.

A POEM IN TEN BOOKS.

By Robert Pollok, A.M.

" Of deep and hallowed impress, full of noble thoughts and graphic conceptions—the production of a mind alive to the great relations of being, and the sublime simplicity of our religion."—*Blackwood's Magazine.*

---o---

LAYS OF THE SCOTTISH CAVALIERS,
AND OTHER POEMS.

By W. Edmondstoune Aytoun,
Professor of Rhetoric and Belles Lettres in the University of Edinburgh.

Eighth Edition, Foolscap Octavo, 7s. 6d.

" Finer ballads than these, we are bold to say, are not to be found in the language."—*Times.*

" Professor Aytoun's ' Lays of the Scottish Cavaliers'—a volume of verse which shows that Scotland has yet a poet. Full of the true fire, it now stirs and swells like a trumpet note— now sinks in cadences sad and wild as the wail of a Highland dirge."—*Quarterly Review.*

---o---

Elegantly printed in Small Octavo, price 5s.

FIRMILIAN; OR, THE STUDENT OF
BADAJOZ.

A SPASMODIC TRAGEDY.

By T. Percy Jones.

" Humour of a kind most rare at all times, and especially in the present day, runs through every page, and passages of true poetry and delicious versification prevent the continual play of sarcasm from becoming tedious."—*Literary Gazette.*

" But we must leave our readers to unravel this mystery for themselves. Enough has been said and sung to make them acquainted with the claims of ' Firmilian,' to be deemed ' the finest poem of the age.' "—*Dublin University Magazine.*

WORKS OF PROFESSOR WILSON.

EDITED BY HIS SON-IN-LAW,

Professor Ferrier.

Now Published, Volumes I. and II. of

THE NOCTES AMBROSIANÆ.

To be completed in Four Volumes, price 6s. each.

"And now a word or two in conclusion about these Ambrosian Nights. It is not too much to say that they are the finest dialogues that ever have been written, except those of Plato, and with these they do not come into comparison. Plato gives us the feast of reason, North the flow of soul. It detracts a little from their popularity that they are written in the Doric of Scotland; while, on the other hand, this very peculiarity, if mastered, adds to their piquancy. . . . . The result is a series of dialogues, in exuberance of life delightful, in dramatic truth perfect, full of the most salient descriptions, the most searching criticism, withering satire, manly pathos, and broadest humour."—*The Times.*

WORKS OF SAMUEL WARREN, D.C.L.

A Cheap Edition in 5 Vols., price 24s. bound in cloth, viz.:—

VOL. I. DIARY OF A LATE PHYSICIAN, 5s. 6d.
VOLS. II. & III. TEN THOUSAND A-YEAR, 2 vols., 9s.
VOL. IV. NOW AND THEN, &c., 4s. 6d.
VOL. V. MISCELLANIES, 5s.

THE
WORKS OF DR THOMAS M'CRIE.

A New and Uniform Edition,

Edited by his Son.

To be completed in Four Vols., Crown Octavo. Vol. I. is now published, containing

THE LIFE OF JOHN KNOX,

With PORTRAITS of KNOX and QUEEN MARY.

Price 6s. bound in cloth.

The remaining Volumes will contain—

VOL. II. LIFE OF ANDREW MELVILLE.
VOL. III. HISTORY OF THE REFORMATION IN SPAIN AND IN ITALY.
VOL. IV. SERMONS AND MISCELLANEOUS WORKS.

In the Press,

INDEX TO THE FIRST FIFTY VOLUMES
OF BLACKWOOD'S MAGAZINE.

In One Volume Octavo.

ESSAYS; HISTORICAL, POLITICAL, AND
MISCELLANEOUS.
By Sir Archibald Alison, Bart., D.C.L.

Three Volumes Demy Octavo, 45s.

" They stamp him as one of the most learned, able, and accomplished writers of the age.
. . . . . . His Essays are a splendid supplement to his History, and the two combined
exhibit his intellect in all its breadth and beauty."—*Dublin University Magazine.*

Foolscap Octavo, 5s.

LECTURES ON THE POETICAL LITERATURE
OF THE PAST HALF-CENTURY.
By D. M. Moir (Δ).

" A delightful volume."—*Morning Chronicle.*
" Exquisite in its taste and generous in its criticisms."—*Hugh Miller.*

POETICAL WORKS OF D. M. MOIR (Δ).
WITH PORTRAIT, AND MEMOIR BY THOMAS AIRD.
Two Volumes Foolscap Octavo, 14s.

" These are volumes to be placed on the favourite shelf, in the familiar nook that holds the
books we love, which we take up with pleasure and lay down with regret."—*Edinburgh
Courant.*

POETICAL WORKS OF THOMAS AIRD.
A New Edition, complete in One Volume, Small Octavo.
In the Press.

Second Edition, Crown Octavo, 10s. 6d.

THE POEMS AND BALLADS OF SCHILLER.
Translated by Sir Edward Bulwer Lytton, Bart.

" The translations are executed with consummate ability. The technical difficulties
attending a task so great and intricate have been mastered or eluded with a power
and patience quite extraordinary; and the public is put in possession of perhaps the best
translation of a foreign poet which exists in our language. Indeed, we know of none so
complete and faithful."—*Morning Chronicle.*

LADY LEE'S WIDOWHOOD.

By Lieut.-Col. E. B. Hamley,
Captain, R.A.

Two Vols. Post Octavo, 21s., with 13 Illustrations by the Author.

———o———

ZAIDEE: A ROMANCE.

By Mrs Oliphant.

In Three Volumes, Post Octavo, price £1, 11s. 6d.

———o———

KATIE STEWART: A TRUE STORY.

Second Edition, in Foolscap Octavo, with Frontispiece and Vignette, 6s.

"A singularly characteristic Scottish story, most agreeable to read and pleasant to recollect. The charm lies in the faithful and life-like pictures it presents of Scottish character and customs, and manners, and modes of life."—*Tait's Magazine.*

———o———

Second Edition, Post Octavo, price 10s. 6d.

THE QUIET HEART.

By the Author of "Katie Stewart."

"We cannot omit our emphatic tribute to 'The Quiet Heart,' a story which, with its deep clear insight, its gentle but strengthening sympathies, and its pictures so delicately drawn, has captivated numerous readers and will confer on many a memory a good and pleasant influence."—*Excelsior.*

———o———

THE MOTHER'S LEGACIE TO HER
UNBORNE CHILDE.

By Elizabeth Joceline.
EDITED BY THE VERY REV. PRINCIPAL LEE.
32mo, 4s. 6d.

"This beautiful and touching legacie."—*Athenæum.*
"A delightful monument of the piety and high feeling of a truly noble mother."—*Morning Advertiser.*

Two Volumes, foolscap, price 12s.

THE DIARY OF A LATE PHYSICIAN.

By Samuel Warren, D.C.L., F.R.S.

" We know of no book in the English language so calculated to rivet the attention and awaken the purest and deepest sympathies of the heart. The man who has not read these tales has yet to learn a lesson in the mysteries of human nature." — *Oxford and Cambridge Review.*

— o —

Three Volumes, foolscap, price 18s.

TEN THOUSAND A-YEAR.

By Samuel Warren, D.C.L., F.R.S.

" ' Ten Thousand a-Year' is perhaps destined in British literature to some such rank as ' Don Quixote ' holds in Spain."—*American Journal.*

— o —

Foolscap, price 6s.

NOW AND THEN.

By Samuel Warren, D.C.L., F.R.S.

" A vindication, in beautiful prose, of the ' ways of God to Man.' A grander moral is not to be found than that which dwells upon the reader's mind when the book is closed— conveyed, too, as it is, in language as masculine and eloquent as any the English tongue can furnish."—*Times.*

— o —

Foolscap, bound in cloth, gilt edges, 5s.

THE LILY AND THE BEE.

By Samuel Warren, D.C.L., F.R.S.

" It is a great theme treated by a masculine intellect enriched with all the resources of varied knowledge, of profound thought, of a highly poetical temperament, and of solemn religious convictions, and enhanced by the graces and the terrors of a command of language absolutely inexhaustible, and in its combinations almost magical."—*Dublin Warder.*

— o —

Two Volumes, Post Octavo, price 24s.

MISCELLANIES: CRITICAL, IMAGINATIVE,
AND JURIDICAL.

By Samuel Warren, D.C.L., F.R.S.

" One of the most readable books we have met with for a long time, and deserves a prominent place in every selected library of modern authorship."—*Manchester Courier.*

CHEAP EDITIONS OF POPULAR WORKS.

LIGHTS AND SHADOWS OF SCOTTISH LIFE.
Foolscap 8vo, 2s. 6d.

THE TRIALS OF MARGARET LYNDSAY.
By the Author of "Lights and Shadows of Scottish Life." Foolscap 8vo, 2s. 6d.

THE FORESTERS.
By the Author of "Lights and Shadows of Scottish Life." Foolscap 8vo, 2s. 6d.

TOM CRINGLE'S LOG.
Complete in One Volume, Foolscap 8vo, 3s. 6d.

THE CRUISE OF THE MIDGE.
By the Author of "Tom Cringle's Log." In One Volume, Foolscap 8vo, 3s. 6d.

THE LIFE OF MANSIE WAUCH,
TAILOR IN DALKEITH. Foolscap 8vo, 2s. 6d.

THE SUBALTERN.
By the Author of "The Chelsea Pensioners." Foolscap 8vo, 2s. 6d.

PENINSULAR SCENES AND SKETCHES.
By the Author of "The Student of Salamanca." Foolscap 8vo, 2s. 6d.

NIGHTS AT MESS, SIR FRIZZLE PUMPKIN,
AND OTHER TALES. Foolscap 8vo, 2s. 6d.

THE YOUTH AND MANHOOD OF CYRIL THORNTON.
By the Author of "Men and Manners in America." Foolscap 8vo, 3s. 6d.

VALERIUS. A ROMAN STORY.
Foolscap 8vo, 2s. 6d.

REGINALD DALTON.
By the Author of "Valerius." Foolscap 8vo, 3s. 6d.

SOME PASSAGES IN THE HISTORY OF ADAM BLAIR, AND HISTORY OF MATTHEW WALD.
By the Author of "Valerius." Foolscap 8vo, 3s. 6d.

ANNALS OF THE PARISH, AND AYRSHIRE LEGATEES.
By JOHN GALT. Foolscap 8vo, 3s. 6d.

SIR ANDREW WYLIE.
By JOHN GALT. Foolscap 8vo, 3s. 6d.

THE PROVOST, AND OTHER TALES.
By JOHN GALT. Foolscap 8vo, 3s. 6d.

THE ENTAIL.
By JOHN GALT. Foolscap 8vo, 3s. 6d.

LIFE IN THE FAR WEST.
By G. F. RUXTON. A New Edition. Foolscap 8vo, 4s.

☞ *At the prices above mentioned the Books are in Paper Covers. In Cloth the Price is 6d. per Vol. extra.*

Octavo, with Map and other Illustrations, Fourth Edition, 14s.

RUSSIAN SHORES OF THE BLACK SEA IN THE AUTUMN OF 1852.

WITH A VOYAGE DOWN THE VOLGA AND A TOUR THROUGH THE COUNTRY OF THE DON COSSACKS.

By Laurence Oliphant, Esq.
Author of a " Journey to Nepaul," &c.

" The latest and best account of the actual state of Russia."—*Standard.*

" The book bears *ex facie* indisputable marks of the shrewdness, quick-sightedness, candour, and veracity of the author.   It is the production of a gentleman, in the true English sense of the word."—*Daily News.*

———o———

In Octavo, Illustrated with Engravings, price 12s. 6d.,

MINNESOTA AND THE FAR WEST.

By Laurence Oliphant, Esq.,
Late Civil Secretary and Superintendent-General of Indian Affairs in Canada;
Author of " The Russian Shores of the Black Sea," &c.

ORIGINALLY PUBLISHED IN BLACKWOOD'S MAGAZINE.

———o———

Second Edition, Foolscap Octavo, price 4s.

LIFE IN THE FAR WEST.

By G. F. Ruxton, Esq.

" One of the most daring and resolute of travellers. . . . . . . A volume fuller of excitement is seldom submitted to the public."—*Athenæum.*

———o———

Two Volumes Octavo, with Maps, &c., price £1, 10s.

NARRATIVE OF A JOURNEY THROUGH SYRIA AND PALESTINE.

By Lieut. Van De Velde.

" He has contributed much to the knowledge of the country, and the unction with which he speaks of the holy places which he has visited, will commend the book to the notice of all religious readers.   His illustrations of Scripture are numerous and admirable."—*Daily News.*

In Crown Octavo, price 10s. 6d.

INSTITUTES OF METAPHYSIC: THE
THEORY OF KNOWING AND BEING.

By James F. Ferrier, A.B., Oxon.
Professor of Moral Philosophy and Political Economy, St Andrews.

"It is a pleasure to meet with a man who, in these days of half-beliefs and feeble assertions, will venture to speak thus strongly. It is a still greater pleasure to meet with a man of profound thought and astonishing subtlety, who is able to express the most abstruse meanings in the most simple language, and to scatter the light spray of wit and pleasantry over those abysses of thought which lead down to the terrible Domdaniel roots of the ocean. We find it difficult to mention any other English work on metaphysics, with even half its power of thought, which can be compared with it in point of style. 'The Institutes of Metaphysic' is indeed the most suggestive work on the subject that has been published for many a long year, and it is the most readable."—*Daily News.*

———o———

BURNETT TREATISE.
(SECOND PRIZE.)

In One Vol. Octavo, price 10s. 6d.

THEISM:
THE WITNESS OF REASON AND NATURE TO AN ALL-WISE AND BENEFICENT CREATOR.

By the Rev. J. Tulloch, D.D.
Principal and Primarius Professor of Theology, St Mary's College, St Andrews.

———o———

ON THE ORIGIN AND CONNECTION OF
THE GOSPELS OF MATTHEW, MARK, AND LUKE;
WITH SYNOPSIS OF PARALLEL PASSAGES AND CRITICAL NOTES.

By James Smith, Esq. of Jordanhill, F.R.S.
Author of the "Voyage and Shipwreck of St Paul." Medium Octavo, price 16s.

"Displays much learning, is conceived in a reverential spirit, and executed with great skill. . . . . . No public school or college ought to be without it."—*Standard.*

———o———

In Octavo, price 14s.

HISTORY OF THE FRENCH PROTESTANT
REFUGEES.

By Prof. Charles Weiss of the Lycee Buonaparte.

"We have risen from the perusal of Mr Weiss's book with feelings of extreme gratification. The period embraced by this work includes the most heart-stirring times of the eventful History of Protestantism, and is of surpassing interest."—*Britannia.*

DEDICATED BY PERMISSION TO HER MAJESTY.

NOW COMPLETED,

In Two large Volumes Royal Octavo, embellished with 1353 Engravings,

THE BOOK OF THE GARDEN.

By Charles M'Intosh,

Late Curator of the Royal Gardens of His Majesty the King of the Belgians, and latterly of those of His Grace the Duke of Buccleuch, at Dalkeith Palace.

Each Volume may be had separately, viz. :—

I.—ARCHITECTURAL AND ORNAMENTAL. Pp. 776, embellished with 1073 Engravings, price £2, 10s.
II.—PRACTICAL GARDENING. Pp. 876, embellished with 280 Engravings, price £1, 17s. 6d.

"We must congratulate both editor and publishers on the completion of this work, which is every way worthy of the character of all concerned in its publication. The scientific knowledge and great experience of the editor in all that pertains to horticulture, not only as regards cultivation, but as a landscape-gardener and garden architect, has enabled him to produce a work which brings all that is known of the various subjects treated of down to the present time; while the manner in which the work is illustrated merits our highest approval."—*The Florist.*

"Mr M'Intosh's splendid and valuable 'Book of the Garden' is at length complete by the issue of the second volume. It is impossible in a notice to do justice to this work. There is no other within our knowledge at all to compare with it in comprehensiveness and ability; and it will be an indispensable possession for the practical gardener, whether amateur or professional."—*The London Guardian.*

———o———

In Two Volumes Royal Octavo, price £3, handsomely bound in cloth, with upwards of 600 Illustrations.

THE BOOK OF THE FARM.

DETAILING THE LABOURS OF THE

FARMER, FARM-STEWARD, PLOUGHMAN, SHEPHERD, HEDGER, CATTLE-MAN, FIELD-WORKER, AND DAIRY-MAID, AND FORMING A SAFE MONITOR FOR STUDENTS IN PRACTICAL AGRICULTURE.

By Henry Stephens, F.R.S.E.

Corresponding Member of the Société Impériale et Centrale d'Agriculture of France, and of the Royal Agricultural Society of Galicia.

THE EIGHTH THOUSAND.

"The best practical book I have ever met with."—*Professor Johnston.*

"We assure agricultural students that they will derive both pleasure and profit from a diligent perusal of this clear directory to rural labour.   The experienced farmer will perhaps think that Mr Stephens dwells upon some matters too simple or too trite to need explanation; but we regard this as a fault leaning to virtue's side in an instructional book.   The young are often ashamed to ask for an explanation of simple things, and are too often discouraged by an indolent or supercilious teacher if they do.   But Mr Stephens entirely escapes this error, for he indicates every step the young farmer should take, and, one by one, explains their several bearings.   .   .   .   .   We have thoroughly examined these volumes; but to give a full notice of their varied and valuable contents would occupy a larger space than we can conveniently devote to their discussion; we therefore, in general terms, commend them to the careful study of every young man who wishes to become a good practical farmer."—*Times.*

"A work, the excellence of which is too well known to need any remarks of ours."—*Farmers' Magazine.*

THE YESTER DEEP-LAND CULTURE.

Being a Detailed Account of the Method of Cultivation which has been successfully
practised for several years by the Marquess of Tweeddale at Yester.

By Henry Stephens, F.R.S.E.
Author of the "Book of the Farm."

In Small Octavo, with Engravings on Wood, price 4s. 6d.

———o———

ITALIAN IRRIGATION.

A Report on the Agricultural Canals of Piedmont and Lombardy ; addressed to the
Hon. the Directors of the East India Company.

With an Appendix, containing Sketch of the Irrigation System of
Northern and Central India.

By Lieut.-Col. Baird Smith, F.G.S.
Captain, Bengal Engineers.

The Second Edition, in Two Volumes Octavo, with Atlas in Folio, price 30s.

———o———

A New Edition, enlarged.
THE FORESTER.

A PRACTICAL TREATISE ON THE PLANTING AND MANAGEMENT OF
FOREST TREES.

By James Brown, Forester,
Arniston.

Illustrated with 109 Engravings by Branston.   Price 21s.

" Sensible, concise, and useful.   We can refer to this as the book to be recommended."—
Gardeners' Chronicle.
" Mr Brown's excellent work."—*Quarterly Review.*

———o———

In Octavo, price 12s.
THE RURAL ECONOMY OF ENGLAND,
SCOTLAND, AND IRELAND.
By Leonce De Lavergne.

Translated from the French.   With Notes by a Scottish Farmer.

" Some years have elapsed since the appearance of a work on agricultural and social economy which combined in so large a degree as this volume great practical skill and theoretical
knowledge, with the power of taking extended views and seizing the latent truths contained
in the facts observed.   Like all really profound works, the ' Rural Economy ' of M. de
Lavergne is larger than its professed subject ; and those who only expect an exposition of
English agriculture, will also find various social problems discussed and resolved, and a light
thrown on several important economical questions. . . . . When we consider
the fulness of matter, the variety of information, the importance of the subject, and the
vigour and picturesqueness with which the whole is presented to the reader, the ' Rural
Economy of England ' may be pronounced one of the best works on the philosophy of agriculture and of agricultural political economy that has appeared."—*Spectator.*

A New and Enlarged Edition of

THE PHYSICAL ATLAS OF NATURAL PHENOMENA.

By Alex. Keith Johnston, F.R.S.E., F.R.G.S., &c.

Geographer to the Queen.

To be completed in Twelve Parts, price One Guinea each.

" There is no map in this noble Atlas upon which we might not be tempted to write largely. Almost every one suggests a volume of reflection, and suggests it by presenting, in a few hours, accurate truths which it would be the labour of a volume to enforce in words, and by imprinting them, at the same time, upon the memory, with such distinctness that their outlines are not likely afterwards to be effaced. The ' Physical Atlas ' is a somewhat costly work, reckoning it only by its paper; but upon its paper is stamped an amount of knowledge that could scarcely be acquired without the reading of as many books as would cost seven times the price."—*Examiner*, August 12, 1854.

THE PHYSICAL ATLAS.

REDUCED FROM THE IMPERIAL FOLIO FOR THE USE OF COLLEGES, ACADEMIES, AND FAMILIES.

By A. Keith Johnston, F.R.S.E., &c.

In Imperial Quarto, handsomely bound, half-morocco, price £2, 12s. 6d.

" Executed with remarkable care, and is as accurate, and, for all educational purposes, as valuable as the splendid large work (by the same author) which has now a European reputation."—*Eclectic Review.*

This day is Published,

AN ATLAS OF ASTRONOMY.

A complete Series of Illustrations of the Heavenly Bodies, drawn with the greatest care, from Original and Authentic Documents.

By Alex. Keith Johnston, F.R.S.E., F.R.G.S., F.G.S.

Geographer in Ordinary to Her Majesty for Scotland; Author of " The Physical Atlas," &c.

EDITED BY J. R. HIND, F.R.A.S.

Imperial Quarto, half-bound morocco, price 21s.

" For care of drawing, fulness of matter, and beauty of arrangement, we have seen no popular Atlas of Astronomy to compare with this volume. The names of Hind and Johnston on the title-page prepared us for a work of rare excellence; but our satisfaction on comparing its plates—so new, so accurate, and so suggestively shaded,—with the poor diagrams from which boys were expected to learn the starry sciences a few years ago, surpassed expectation. The illustrations are eighteen in number,—lunar, solar, stellar; and are so constructed as to present to the eye a series of lessons in the most captivating of human studies, simple in outline and cumulative in result. To say that Mr Hind's ' Atlas ' is the best thing of the kind is not enough,—it has no competitor."—*Athenæum.*

A NEW MAP OF EUROPE.

By A. Keith Johnston.

The Plates have been engraved in the highest style of art, and besides the Political divisions, show distinctly the more important Physical features. The Navigation Tracks, with the distances of the various ports from each other, in lines of railway on the Continent, and the Key Map, with all the Lines of Magnetic Telegraph brought down to the latest date, will be found of the greatest practical utility.

The Map is fully coloured, and measures 4 feet 2 inches by 3 feet 5 inches.

Price, mounted on Cloth and Mahogany Roller, Varnished, or folded in 4to in a handsome Cloth Case, £2, 2s.

In Two Volumes, Crown Octavo, price 11s. 6d.

THE CHEMISTRY OF COMMON LIFE.

By James F. W. Johnston, M.A., F.R.SS. L. & E., &c.

Author of " Lectures on Agricultural Chemistry and Geology," &c.

With 113 Illustrations on Wood, and a Copious Index.

" All will concur in admiring the profound thought which has ennobled so many familiar things, and has even tinged the commonest processes of household life with the hues of novelty and surprise. The work deserves to be universally read."—*British Quarterly Review.*

" By the simplicity and lucidness of language and arrangement he shows how thoroughly he is master of his subject, and how well qualified he is to open our eyes to behold the wonders of common life, while he conducts us into the laboratory of nature, where we may see her at her own workshop labouring for the good of man—balancing with consummate skill the various influences of air, and earth, and water, for the support of organised exertion. With such a pleasant guide none will refuse to enter into the mysteries of common things, nor spurn those valuable lessons deducible from his teachings."—*Dublin Mail.*

———o———

Preparing for Publication,

A MAP OF THE GEOLOGY OF EUROPE.

By Sir Roderick I. Murchison, D.C.L., M.A., F.R.S.;

AND

James Nicol, F.R.S.E., F.G.S.,

Professor of Natural History, Aberdeen.

On Four Sheets, Imperial Folio.

———o———

A CATECHISM OF PRACTICAL AGRICULTURE.

By Henry Stephens, Esq., F.R.S.E.

Author of the " Book of the Farm."

With Numerous Illustrations, price One Shilling and Sixpence.

———o———

Price One Shilling and Sixpence, bound in cloth.

INTRODUCTORY TEXT-BOOK OF GEOLOGY.

By David Page, F.G.S.

Crown Octavo, pp. 128, with Illustrations.

" Of late it has not often been our good fortune to examine a text-book on science of which we could express an opinion so entirely favourable as we are enabled to do of Mr Page's little work."—*Athenæum.*

———o———

ADVANCED TEXT-BOOK OF GEOLOGY,

DESCRIPTIVE AND INDUSTRIAL.

By David Page, F.G.S.

Crown Octavo, with Illustrations, price 5s.

" The purpose of these Text-Books may be briefly stated: The 'Introductory' is meant to exhibit a general outline of Geology intelligible to beginners, and sufficient for those who wish to become acquainted merely with the leading facts of the science; the 'Advanced,' on the other hand, presents the subject in detail, and is intended for senior pupils, and those who desire to prosecute the study in its principles as well as deductions."

SCHOOL ATLASES

BY

ALEX. KEITH JOHNSTON,

F.R.S.E., F.R.G.S., F.G.S.

Geographer to the Queen, Author of the " Physical Atlas," &c.

I.

PHYSICAL GEOGRAPHY, illustrating, in a series of Original Designs, the Elementary Facts of Geology, Hydrology, Meteorology, and Natural History. In this Atlas of Physical Geography the subject is treated in a more simple and elementary manner than in the previous works of the Author—the object being to convey broad and general ideas on the form and structure of our Planet, and the principal phenomena affecting its outer crust.

II.

CLASSICAL GEOGRAPHY, comprising, in Twenty Plates, Maps and Plans of all the important Countries and Localities referred to by Classical Authors, constructed from the best Materials, and embodying the Results of the most Recent Investigations. Printed in Colours, uniform with the Author's General and Physical School Atlases, and accompanied by a Complete Index of Places, in which the proper Quantities of the Syllables are marked, by T. HARVEY, M.A., Oxon., one of the Classical Masters in the Edinburgh Academy.

III.

GENERAL AND DESCRIPTIVE GEOGRAPHY, exhibiting the Actual and Comparative Extent of all the Countries in the World; with their present Political Divisions. Constructed with a special view to the purposes of Sound Instruction, and presenting the following new features :—1. Enlarged Size, and consequent Distinctness of Plan. 2. The most Recent Improvements in Geography. 3. A Uniform Distinction in Colour between Land and Water. 4. Great Clearness, Uniformity, and Accuracy of Colouring. 5. A ready way of comparing Relative Areas by means of Scales. 6. The insertion of the Corresponding Latitudes of Countries, Towns, &c. 7. References to Colonial Possessions, &c., by Figures and Notes. 8. A carefully compiled and complete Index.

IV.

ASTRONOMY. Edited by J. R. HIND, Esq., F.R.A.S., &c. With Notes and descriptive Letterpress to each Plate, embodying all recent discoveries in Astronomy. Eighteen Maps. Printed in Colours by a new process.

The above are all uniform in size. Price of each Atlas:—In Octavo (for School use), strongly half-bound, 12s. 6d. In a Portfolio, each Map separate, and mounted on canvass, 16s. 6d. In Quarto, half-bound morocco, £1, 1s. Separate Maps mounted on canvass, each 8d.

V.

ELEMENTARY SCHOOL ATLAS OF GENERAL AND DESCRIPTIVE GEOGRAPHY, for the use of Junior Classes ; including a Map of Canaan and Palestine, and a General Index. In Demy Quarto, price 7s. 6d. half-bound.

VI.

A SERIES OF EIGHT GEOGRAPHICAL PROJECTIONS, to accompany KEITH JOHNSTON's Atlases of Physical and General School Geography. Comprising the WORLD (on Mercator's Projection)—EUROPE—ASIA—AFRICA—NORTH AMERICA—SOUTH AMERICA—THE BRITISH ISLES. With a Blank Page for laying down the Meridians and Parallels of any Map by the more advanced Pupils. In a Portfolio, price 2s. 6d.

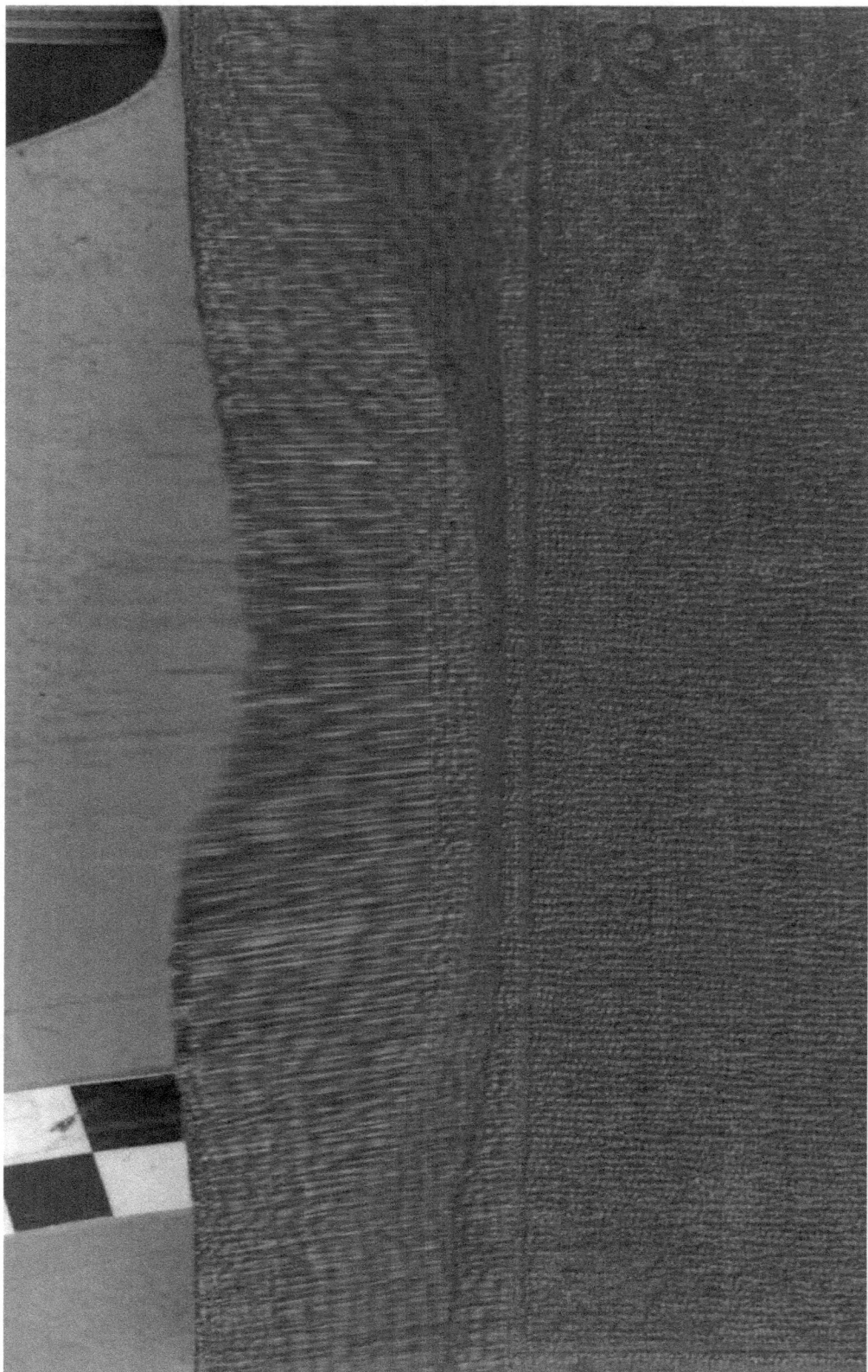

Check Out More Titles From HardPress Classics Series In this collection we are offering thousands of classic and hard to find books. This series spans a vast array of subjects – so you are bound to find something of interest to enjoy reading and learning about.

Subjects:
Architecture
Art
Biography & Autobiography
Body, Mind &Spirit
Children & Young Adult
Dramas
Education
Fiction
History
Language Arts & Disciplines
Law
Literary Collections
Music
Poetry
Psychology
Science
…and many more.

Visit us at www.hardpress.net

CPSIA information can be obtained
at www.ICGtesting.com
Printed in the USA
BVHW060212280819
556849BV00019B/3489/P